Mounting and Using Lace

Mounting
and Using Lace
Jean Withers

DRYAD PRESS LTD, LONDON

ISBN 0 8521 9590 7

Typeset by Servis Filmsetting Ltd, Manchester
and printed in Great Britain by
Anchor Brendon Ltd
Tiptree, Essex
for the publishers
Dryad Press Ltd
4 Fitzhardinge Street, London W1H 0AH

Contents

Acknowledgment

My thanks to all students and friends for their encouragement, but especially to June and Stanley Jackson for the many hours of work in producing the photographs; Helen Jackson for modelling several items; Joan Brimblecombe and June Jackson for checking the manuscript; Dorothy Cox for permission to illustrate lace made on prickings from her book *Making Lace with Little Grey Rabbit*; and my husband John for typing the manuscript and, together with my son Ian, being reasonably patient on those occasions when lace has nearly been served for tea!

Introduction

Bobbin lacemaking has enjoyed a tremendous revival in the last few years, and many people with little or no experience of other crafts have found in it a source of great pleasure. However, when the lace is removed from the pillow there is often a plaintive cry of 'Now what do I do with it?'. This book not only answers that question but also will stimulate lacemakers into seeing their lace as part of a complete article, and to consider combining lace with forms of needlework – it is always worthwhile trying out new ideas.

In the following pages there are ideas for achieving maximum effect from a piece of lace, whether small and simple or more ambitious. Even the most inexperienced lacemaker should be able to successfully utilize her lace in an attractive way; the lace may, of course, be as ambitious as choice and ability allow. A few prickings are included, but detailed working methods are not, as these may be found in the many excellent books now available on the subject. Details of the threads used are given only as a guide.

CHAPTER ONE

Planning, Choosing Materials and Patterns

Having spent a great deal of time on the construction of a piece of lace it is surely worthwhile spending a little extra time when making it up. Do *not* be tempted to machine stitch it into place as this will detract from the lace, and there are those who will immediately assume that the lace must also be machine made. The sewing machine should only be used for stitching which will *not* be seen. An even line of hand-made stitches can be achieved with a little practice. If you are unfamiliar with a particular stitch, first work a small practice line on a spare piece of fabric; in any event this is always worthwhile because you will then have checked that you are using a suitable size of stitch and thread to achieve the required effect on your chosen fabric.

Before starting work, read carefully through the method, so that you will have an idea of what you are trying to achieve; then read through each step carefully as you come to work it. If you are unfamiliar with a technique, try something fairly simple first. A simple well-made item is preferable to something which is ambitious yet badly done, and will give you confidence to proceed further. Bear in mind, also, that small does not necessarily mean easy to make. Often a large item will be easier to handle because a deeper hem can be used and any corner mitres will therefore be easier to make.

Many of the problems associated with finishing and mounting lace are best considered before the piece is started. You will spend many hours making it so it is well worth planning ahead and working samples to check that the lace will

be suitable. However, once you have started work, do not be inflexible but allow your ideas to develop as work proceeds.

When planning, the first consideration should be the suitability of the finished item for its purpose. For example, table linen should be easy to launder and of a fairly bold design which will both look well from a distance and be interesting on closer inspection. A fine Bucks point pattern would not be suitable in this case whereas a coarser torchon pattern would be very effective.

Having decided on the item to be made and the type and weight of lace to be used, it is now time to select a suitable pricking. Your choice will depend to a certain extent upon the intended method of construction of the finished article. For example, if the ends of the lace can be enclosed in a fabric seam, no further finishing will be required and there will be a wide choice of possible prickings. Nor will the ends of thread create a problem on a piece of lace which is to be applied to fabric where the ends may be taken through to the back of the work.

In these cases any attractive pricking of a suitable scale may be chosen, but when planning a closed border or a motif for insertion, consideration should be given to the placing of the join and the method of dealing with the ends of thread.

There are a number of ways of dealing with the ends of thread on a closed border and sometimes it is possible to use more than one on a particular piece of lace. It is usually preferable to attach the lace to the fabric before dealing with the ends. This gives you more to handle, helps prevent the lace from being pulled out of shape, and also allows all the ends from the edge and footside pairs to be darned away into the fabric rather than into the lace.

When ends must be darned into the lace there are several possibilities. For a fairly coarse torchon lace often the best method of hiding the ends is to darn them back into adjacent areas of cloth stitch (see figs. 55 and 66). Forming the ends into a roll on the back of the lace and overcasting it to the back of a gimp or area of cloth stitch is successful for fine laces, but will be bulky and tend to show even from the right side of a coarser one. For this reason a closed border in a coarse torchon lace is best worked on a pricking which incorporates reasonably large areas of cloth stitch; start working the lace with those areas. A half stitch trail and large areas of ground will be virtually impossible to join invisibly in lace made with a coarse thread.

It is also possible to overcast two ends (one at a time) to the back of the legs of a spider and then darn them into the back of the body. Threads may also be oversewn (again, one at a time) to the back of the twisted passive pairs in a twisted torchon fan (see fig. 66). It is sometimes possible to darn the ends of thread into leaves and tallies alongside the passive threads, or alternatively they may form a small roll which is overcast to the back of the leaf (see fig. 15).

The most inconspicuous join can be made by dispersing the threads by darning them away in as many directions as possible and then forming those which cannot be darned away into a roll. The threads can form more than one roll, and bulk will be reduced if the threads can be rolled in different directions (see fig. 32).

When the ends of the lace are neither to be joined nor enclosed they must be started and finished with a made up edge. There are a variety of ways of achieving this (see books on lace technique) but one of the simplest and strongest is to choose a pricking which includes cloth stitch fans and diamonds. The strip is started and finished with these areas of cloth stitch which may then be folded back and neatly hemmed in place, enclosing all the short ends. Both ends of

the strip of lace are handled in the same way so that they will match exactly. This method was used for the strips of lace on the place mat illustrated in fig. 60.

Several things must be borne in mind when choosing the fabric to which the lace is to be attached. As the fabric and lace will be laundered together, they should be of fibres which need similar treatment. This is most easily achieved by using fabric and thread of the same composition, for example, linen lace on linen fabric (although cotton lace is successful on linen fabric). Some polyester/cotton mixtures are very useful for such things as placemats which will be frequently laundered, but because of their easy-care qualities they can sometimes be more difficult to work with because they do not readily take a crease. If possible choose those fabrics with a low polyester content.

In the past most lace was made with linen or cotton threads because these were readily available and easy to work. When making 'heirlooms' today these threads are certainly the best choice. However, some threads of man-made fibres will work up successfully and it is always worth experimenting with them.

Whatever fibres are chosen, the fabric should be of the correct scale so that the lace appears to 'grow' from the fabric. The best general guide is that the cloth stitch areas of the lace and the woven fabric should appear to be the same. If the lace contains no cloth stitch areas then the fabric should appear to be woven from the same thread; the eye gives a reasonable amount of latitude in this respect. Always use the best materials you can afford.

The traditional colours for lace are white, ecru and black; but it is well worthwhile experimenting with colours providing that these do not swamp the 'laciness' of the lace. Edgings worked in pastel tints can be very effective if attached to the same coloured fabric or a fabric of a deeper shade. When the lace and fabric are supposed to be the same colour they should be an *exact* match; if this is not possible it is usually better to choose a colour which is clearly different. White and black can often be the most difficult colours to match. Remember that the colour of your thread can appear slightly different when it has been made into lace (not just because it is dirty!).

Where the working of the lace permits, a deeper or paler shade of thread may be used as a weaver. This is particularly effective in a torchon fan where a thread of a contrasting colour could also be used, but this must be chosen with great care. A piece of lace in a pale colour applied over a deeper shade fabric, or vice versa, can also be very attractive. Do not, however, overlook the effectiveness of lace applied over a self-coloured fabric, where the interest will lie in the textures of lace and fabric (see fig. 114).

When the lace pricking and fabric have been chosen, it is then possible to choose the most suitable method of mounting the lace for its intended purpose.

CHAPTER TWO

Using Frames and Mounts

A lot of modern lace is mounted in picture frames, gilt and silverware and under paperweights. The methods for using the gilt and silverware are included in the pack and the use of picture frames is fairly evident. There are a few points, however, which are worth emphasising.

The fabric to which the lace will be attached must be carefully chosen so that its texture does not overwhelm the lace. Felt is often a good choice; it is easily handled, available in a wide range of colours and the modern ones, made of synthetic fibres, usually have a pleasant sheen which enhances the lace. Paper and card are suitable backing materials which are often overlooked, and again a wide choice of colour is available.

The lace is applied invisibly to the fabric as described on page 50, using only a few stitches. A pile fabric such as velvet will need very careful handling to prevent it and the lace from distorting each other. The stitches holding the lace in place must be loose enough not to pull the lace down into the pile and care must be taken to ensure that the glass of the frame does not flatten the pile, thus covering parts of the lace. To avoid this happening, cut thin strips of card and place them between the glass and the fabric round the edges where they will not show beneath the frame.

To attach the lace to paper or card, take a matching thread up through the paper, over a thread of the lace and down again through the same hole. These two ends of thread may then be held in place at the back with sticky tape. Repeat where necessary to prevent the lace from slipping. If required, any ends of thread from the lace may also be taken through to the back of the paper, although if there are a lot it is better to finish them into the lace first, to avoid weakening the paper.

The mounting fabric is best cut to the required size and shape after the lace has been attached to it. Card, felt or other materials which will not fray may be cut to the exact size required. Other fabrics will need different treatment; there is a choice of two methods. If the fabric will stand the necessary heat and pressing, a piece of iron-on interfacing may be bonded to the fabric before cutting it to the exact size required. Alternatively, cut a piece of thin card to the required size and then place it on top of the fabric (face down) on the table. Fold the edges to the back and stick into place, taking care that the front of the fabric is lying smoothly and that the lace is in its correct position. If the fabric is bulky, trim away the excess layers at the corners to keep them as flat as possible, and if the outer edge is curved it will be necessary to clip the turnings at intervals to enable them to lie flat. As an alternative to glueing, the fabric could be laced into place (see page 17).

When choosing a frame (or any other sort of mount) do *not* use one into which the lace will only just fit; it needs space around it in order to be shown to advantage. If the next size of available

fig. 1 *A variety of frames, three of which illustrate the use of 'windows'.*

frame is too large, cut a window in a piece of card or thick paper, of an appropriate size for your lace. This gives scope for a variety of window shapes (not necessarily geometric or symmetrical) to show your lace to advantage and can overcome the problem of finding the right shape of frame. For example, it is often difficult to find the correct frame for an oval piece of lace. When planning the shape of the window, bear in mind that one with straight sides will be easier to cut accurately (against a steel rule) than other shapes, which will have to be cut freely with a steady hand. Also remember that in a rectangular picture frame, the border at the lower edge should be larger than the other three (this is also true if the lace is not mounted in a window).

The colour of this card can be chosen to enhance the overall effect; a lighter or darker shade of the colour of the background fabric is often successful. By cutting a progressively larger window in each, more than one layer of card could be used, resulting in a feeling of depth which is increased by using graded shades of one colour (fig. 1 illustrates lace mounted in frames with 'windows' and fig. 2 shows the various layers used in the frame).

Great care must be taken when cutting these windows. The shape must be accurate and the edge should be cleanly cut with a sharp craft knife, using a steel rule for any straight edges. A crisper appearance may be given to the mount by drawing a fine line a little way from the edge of the window to surround it, using a suitable coloured ink.

The card window mount could also be covered with fabric. Choose one which will not fray easily or overpower the lace. The working method is as follows:

Cut away the fabric for the window, leaving turnings of about 10mm (⅜in.) and clipping them at intervals so that they will lie flat when turned back. Lay the material face down on a flat, clean surface and then place the prepared card into position on top of it, leaving a margin of fabric round the outer edges of the card. Smear fabric glue (e.g. Copydex) over the inner edge of the back of the card and then fold back the fabric turnings, smoothing them carefully into place so that there is a neat fold of material over the edge of the card. Take particular care with the corners of squares and rectangles where the turning must be clipped right into the corner. On the outer edge fold the fabric back over the card and glue it into place, taking care that the fabric lies smoothly over the front of the card and is not marked with glue. If required, a layer of wadding, cut to the exact size of the card, may be included between the card and fabric.

A variety of picture frames are available, and with the use of window mounts it should be possible to find something to suit. If not, it is possible to make a fabric-covered frame which can be completely original. Whatever fabric or embroidery technique is chosen, it should echo your lace and not overpower it.

Some suggestions for suitable fabrics are:

(a) A plain colour with an interesting but delicate texture.
(b) A very soft leather.
(c) A delicate piece of embroidery.
(d) A fabric which has been spray-dyed or painted.

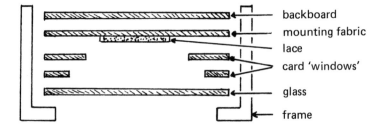

backboard
mounting fabric
lace
card 'windows'
glass
frame

fig. 2 *Cross-section of frame showing position of two 'windows'.*

(e) Canvas work embroidery on a fine canvas. This is particularly attractive if it is carried out in one colour, relying on the textures of the different stitches for its effect.

(f) A smooth fabric quilted in a pattern to complement the lace. The pattern for the frame illustrated in fig. 3 is shown actual size in fig. 5 and the working methods are described below and on page 79.

The fabric may be sprayed with a fabric waterproofer to help keep it clean. This treatment is possible on many fabrics but always try it first on a sample to check that it will not have an adverse effect on your fabric and threads.

To make the frame, first decide on its finished size and shape; squares and rectangles will be easier to make but it is worth experimenting with others. Cut a piece of firm card to the chosen size and then cut the required window from it.

If the fabric is to be embroidered or painted, mark out the design area with tacking stitches using the card as a template. Do remember that some embroidery techniques, especially quilting, will tend to 'shrink' the fabric. Work the embroidery and then, if the fabric is to be waterproofed, spray it at this stage.

The fabric may now be stuck to the inner edges of the window as described on page 14 but the generous margins round the outer edges are left free for the time being. If canvas work has been chosen, the canvas will fray badly when cut and will be difficult to handle on the inner edge. One possible solution is to work the embroidery up to, but not beyond, the inner finished edge. A binding could then be machined along this line

fig. 3 *Quilted frame*

and be taken to the back of the card and stuck into place, completely out of sight. If the fabric is quilted, cut away the wadding from the turnings.

Next, place a piece of picture glass (or sheet acetate), cut to size, on top of the card, having first covered the edges of the glass with masking tape to prevent them from cutting the fabric – and your fingers. Make sure that the glass or acetate is perfectly clean, especially on the inside which will not be accessible later. Fig. 4 shows the various layers in the frame.

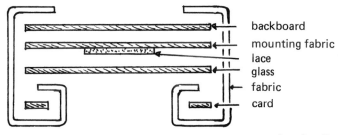

backboard
mounting fabric
lace
glass
fabric
card

fig. 4 *Cross-section of fabric frame showing the various layers.*

fig. 5 *Pattern and pricking for frame and lace illustrated in fig. 3.*

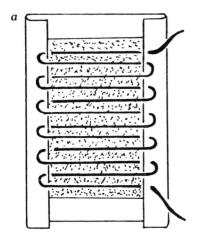

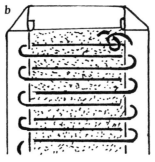

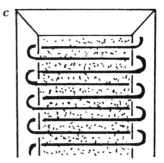

fig. 6 *Lacing fabric over a square or rectangle:* ***a*** *Lace opposite sides together.* ***b*** *Fold in corners.* ***c*** *Fold fabric edges to back of card.*

Now attach the lace to the backing fabric, cut it to size as described on page 12 and then place it face down on top of the glass. For the back of the frame place a piece of firm card, cut to shape, on top of the pile. The frame may now be completed by folding the edges of the front fabric over to the back and glueing or lacing them into place. In this case, lacing will give a stronger finish and enable you to tuck in the raw edges as you work.

To lace the fabric, use a strong thread long enough to complete the lacing, and take stitches on opposite sides as shown in fig. 6a. (If you start at the centre, the length of thread will be more easily managed.) Pull these stitches up tightly, one by one, when they are all in place and fasten off the thread very securely, knotting it if possible. The opposite edges are then laced in the same way, keeping the corners as neat and flat as

possible by folding in the edges as shown in figs. 6b and 6c. If a circle or oval is to be laced, start by working running stitches round the edge with a strong thread. This thread is then pulled up tightly before lacing across the shape as shown in figs. 7a and 7b. The back of the frame may then be neatened by stitching a piece of fabric to it.

To hang the frame, stitch a metal eye or loop to each side at the back and tie string firmly into these loops. Alternatively, the frame could stand in a small plate stand.

fig. 7 *Lacing fabric over a circle or oval:* ***a*** *Work running stitch round outer edge.* ***b*** *Gather up to fit over card, fasten off and lace from side to side.*

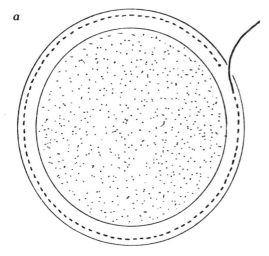

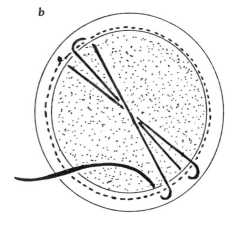

17

fig. 8 *Plastic pen pot.*

Bookmarks are another popular choice with lacemakers and are more durable if they are inserted into a plastic case or mounted on ribbon.

If the lace is mounted on stiff paper or thin card it will be much easier to insert into a plastic case. Cut the paper longer than the case and twice its width. It is then scored down the centre and folded in half, making it the correct width to slide into the case. Open the paper out, so that the lace may be fastened invisibly to one side of it (see page 12) at the top and bottom. When the card is slipped back into the case, the end of the card and case are cut off together to the required length.

When ribbon is being used, choose a fairly lightweight one which may be pressed, and cut a piece twice the required length. Stitch the lace into place (see page 50) at one end of the ribbon and darn any unwanted ends to the back. Then fold the ribbon in half, enclosing a length of hemming web (available from haberdashers), and press according to the instructions on the packet to bond the two layers of ribbon together. This bonding will help to stiffen the ribbon, the ends of which may now be cut to the chosen shape.

It is always worth keeping an eye open for items which may be used for displaying lace. The plastic penpot in fig. 8 originally contained a printed calendar; this was removed and replaced with lace mounted on card. This was simply done by folding the ends of the lace over the card at top and bottom and holding them in place with sticky tape. With a little imagination other items could doubtless be found.

18

CHAPTER THREE

Methods of Attaching Lace Edgings to Fabric

There are a number of ways of attaching lace to fabric; most of them fall into one of two categories:

(a) Direct methods where the fabric is finished and the lace attached in one operation.
(b) Indirect methods where the fabric hem is finished first and the lace attached later.

The method chosen for a particular piece of work will depend upon several things. The type and weight of the lace and fabric, the shape required and the intended purpose of the finished item are the main points to consider. For example, heavier laces need to be attached to firm hems which will withstand the pull on them. The same is also true of items which will be frequently laundered. Tiny pieces of fabric (especially circles and irregular shapes) are difficult to hem whilst retaining an accurate shape, so that in these situations one of the direct methods would be easier to manage.

The direct methods (three-sided and four-sided stitch in particular) are difficult to undo without damage to the lace, so if it is likely to outwear the fabric or need to be removed at a later date, these methods are best avoided. If however for other reasons (e.g. shape or size) they are the most desirable, consider using a narrow lace braid to which the lace is later attached (see page 28).

Whichever method is chosen, if the piece of lace has a straight edge then it must exactly follow the straight grain of the fabric (for hexagons and octagons, of course, only some of the sides can).

When placing the lace, right side up, onto the right side of the fabric, check that it is the correct shape; circles should be truly circular and may be checked by measuring the diameter in several places. For small and irregular shapes it can sometimes be helpful to make a paper template by taking a rubbing of the pricking and cutting out just inside the footside pinholes. This will serve as a guide; your lace may be slightly smaller as it will tend to relax when it is taken off the pillow.

The thread used for making the lace is usually suitable for attaching it to the fabric, ensuring a perfect match (and using up some of the thread left on the bobbins!). *Never* start with a knot – always darn the thread into the hem or behind the stitching.

DIRECT METHODS

(1) Buttonhole stitch (figs. 9 and 10)
This method is suitable on firmly woven fabrics where the stitching cannot pull away in use. It is ideal for small circles and for irregularly shaped pieces of lace and can also be used for squares or rectangles. A fine thread should be chosen for the stitching, otherwise the finished result can appear rather heavy.

Cut a piece of fabric larger than the required finished size and pin the lace into place. Using a small running stitch and a matching thread, tack the lace into position, keeping the tacking close to the footside edge. This tacking may be left in position and will help to strengthen the edge.

Now work buttonhole stitch (see fig. 11) with the looped edge facing towards the headside of the lace. Just cover the footside edge threads of

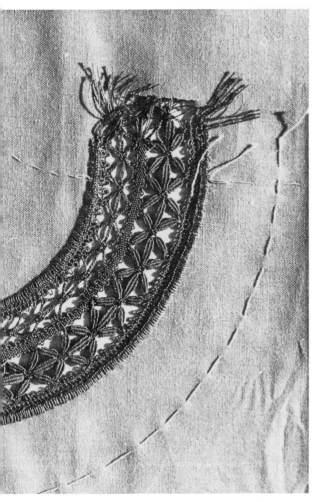

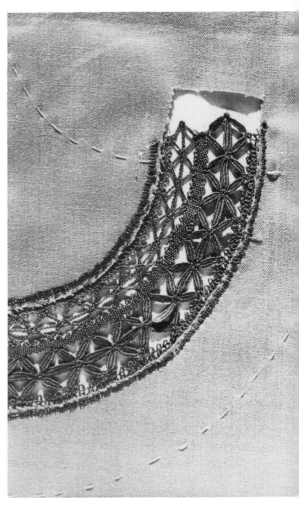

fig. 9 *Detail of patch pocket illustrated in fig. 110. Right side shows buttonhole stitch to attach lace. Actual width of lace 29mm ($1\frac{1}{8}$in.).*

fig. 10 *Detail of patch pocket. Wrong side shows fabric cut away close to stitching.*

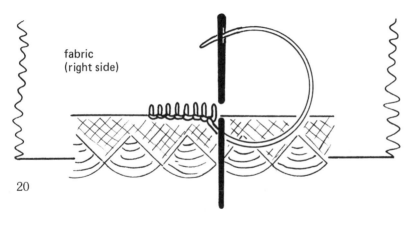

fabric
(right side)

fig. 11 *Buttonhole stitch to attach lace directly to fabric. Stitches are shown spaced, for clarity, but should touch each other.*

the lace and the tacking thread but take care *not* to enclose footside passive pairs. When the stitching is complete, cut away the surplus fabric from the back of the lace as close to the stitching as possible, being careful not to cut the lace or the stitches.

(2) Three-sided stitch (figs. 12 and 23)

This is extremely difficult to undo because, when finished, the stitches should be virtually invisible. It will also mark the material permanently, so it is worth checking carefully that it is correctly positioned. If used on loosely woven fabric it may pull away but it is ideal for use with finely woven ones, especially where curved or irregular shapes are needed. This stitch belongs to the pulled-fabric group of stitches, the decorative effect being produced by the pattern of the holes, not the stitches. To obtain this effect, use a fine thread and a large, blunt needle that will not split the threads of the fabric but will go between them. A No. 24 tapestry needle will be suitable for a fine fabric.

Tack the lace into place on the fabric and then stitch it as shown in fig. 13, taking in only the footside edge pairs of the lace. Each stitch must be pulled tightly to form holes and the fabric must be held taut while working to prevent puckering. For tiny pieces and irregular shapes you may find it easier to stretch the fabric in an embroidery frame or tack it to stiff paper (if you are working over paper, take care to stitch only through the fabric and not the paper).

Normally each stitch should be the same length, but when working round curves this will have to be adjusted slightly to accommodate the curve (see fig. 13j). If the stitch is following the grain of the fabric, make sure it does so exactly. When the stitching is complete, carefully cut away the surplus fabric from the back of the lace. It may be cut as close to the stitching as possible or a short distance away, in which case the edge is then overcast closely on the wrong side, for neatness and strength.

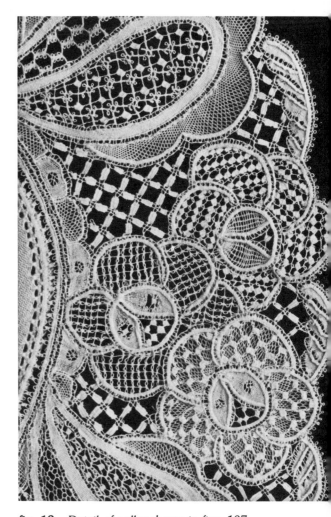

fig. 12 *Detail of collar shown in figs. 107 and 108. Right side shows narrow lace braid attached with three-sided stitch and lace overcast to braid. Minimum actual depth of lace is 57mm (2¼in.).*

a

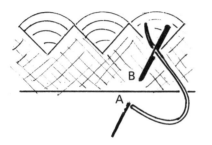

b

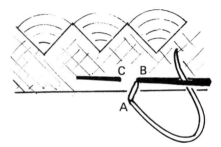

c

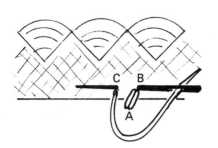

d

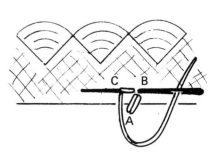

e

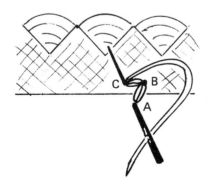

f

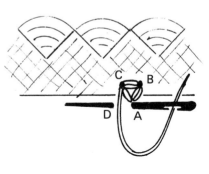

g

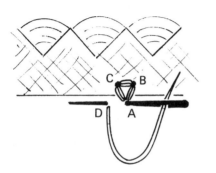

h

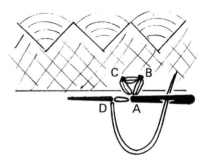

22

i

j

fig. 13 *Three-sided stitch. Pull each stitch tight.* ***a*** *Come up at A, in at B and back up at A.* ***b*** *Go in at B and come up at C.* ***c*** *Go in at B and come up at C.* ***d*** *Go in at B and come up at C.* ***e*** *Go in at A and come up at C.* ***f*** *Go in at A and come up at D.* ***g*** *Go in at A and come up at D.* ***h*** *Go in at A and come up at D.* ***i*** *Repeat* ***a*** *to* ***h*** *to make a line of stitches.* ***j*** *Adjust length of stitches to work round a curve.*

(3) Four-sided stitch (figs. 14 and 15)

This is another pulled-fabric stitch and is used in the same situations; it has the same advantages and disadvantages as three-sided stitch. It may be more likely to pull away than three-sided stitch because each side of the square is formed by a single stitch, not a double one. For a purely decorative effect it may be worked on a single layer of fabric.

The method of working the stitch is shown in fig. 16, again pulling each stitch tight and holding the fabric taut (see three-sided stitch).

fig. 14 *Right side to show four-sided stitch. Actual depth of lace 19mm (¾in.). (The pricking for this lace appears in* Making Lace with Little Grey Rabbit *by Dorothy Cox.)*

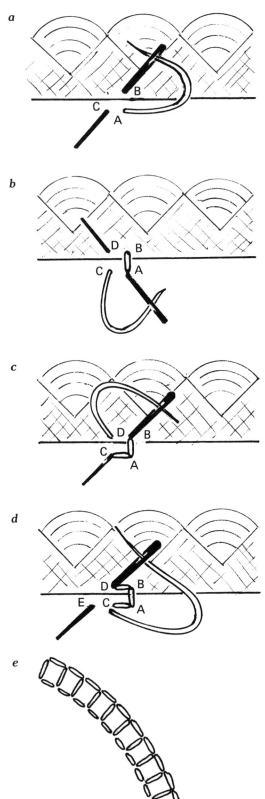

fig. 15 *Wrong side of fig. 14. Note the threads rolled up the back of the leaves on the left-hand side of the complete 'flower'.*

fig. 16 (right) *Four-sided stitch. Pull each stitch tight.* **a** *Come up at A, go in at B and come out at C.* **b** *Go in at A and out at D.* **c** *Go in at B and come out at C.* **d** *Go in at D and come out at E, ready for the next stitch.* **e** *Adjust the length of stitches to work round a curve. The stitch should form a line of crosses on the reverse.*

(4) Pin stitch (figs. 17 and 18)

This is yet another of the pulled-fabric stitches, and the same considerations apply as for three-sided stitch. When the sewing is complete, cut the fabric a little way from the stitching and then overcast the edge to form a tiny roll at the back of the work. If it is cut close to the stitches, it is likely to pull away.

fig. 17 (below left)   *Pin stitch used to attach lace. Actual width of lace 26mm (1in.). (The pricking for this lace appears in* Making Lace with Little Grey Rabbit *by Dorothy Cox.)*

fig. 18   *Wrong side of fig. 17. Note the cut edge of fabric has been overcast.*

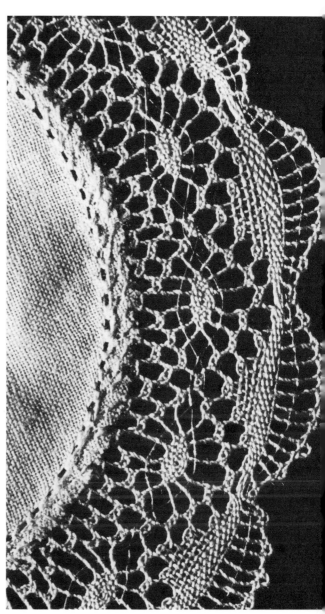

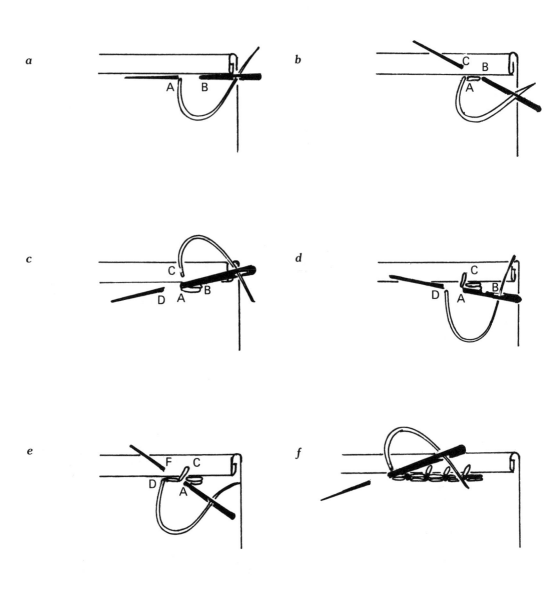

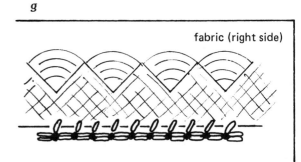

fig. 19 *Pin stitch.* **a** *Come up at A, go in at B and out again at A. Pull tight.* **b** *Go in at B and out at C. Pull tight.* **c** *Go in at A and out at D.* **d** *Go in at A and out at D. Pull tight.* **e** *Go in at A and out at F. Pull tight.* **f** *Repeat* **c**, **d** *and* **e** *along row.* **g** *Position of stitches when attaching lace directly to fabric.*

fabric (right side)

This stitch is more useful as a method of stitching down a hem, as shown in figs. 19a to 19f. The placing of the stitch when it is used to attach lace directly is shown in fig. 19g. If the effect of a drawn thread hem is required but the threads are too fine to draw, or if the edge is curved, pin stitch is an excellent choice. It is also useful as a purely decorative stitch.

(5) Overcasting

This is another method which requires a firmly woven fabric that will not pull away from the stitching. There are two methods of working; the first may be used for any shape, but the second, whilst resulting in a stronger finish, is best suited to straight-sided articles.

Method 1: Tack the lace into position on the fabric using a matching thread which may be left in place. The footside edge of the lace is then covered with a close overcasting stitch as shown in fig. 20. Each stitch should touch the preceding one and pass right through the fabric. When the stitching is complete the excess fabric at the back is cut away close to the stitching.

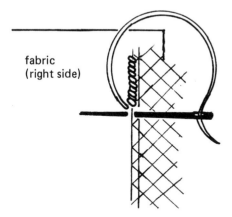

fig. 20   *Close overcasting stitch.*

Method 2: Prepare a single fold hem as described on page 31; mitre the corners if necessary. Using a matching thread, tack the lace to the folded edge with an open overcasting stitch following the instructions on page 30. Then, working from the right side, work the close overcasting as above making each stitch right through the fold of the fabric. Finally cut the excess fabric away from the back, close to the stitching.

(6) Cording

This is worked in a similar way to overcasting by either of the methods described above. The corded effect, which also strengthens the edge, is obtained by laying a thicker matching thread or fine cord over the edge of the lace and enclosing it with the overcasting stitches as shown in fig. 21.

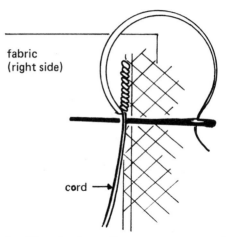

fig. 21   *Cording. Close overcasting stitch is worked over a cord.*

Be particularly careful to make each stitch right through the fabric and over the footside edge of the lace. If a suitable thick thread is not available, several strands of the lace thread may be twisted together to make a fine cord. This was done on the handkerchief illustrated in fig. 22, which was worked by method 2.

Where the cord joins, its ends should be spliced as follows. Untwist each end for a short distance, cut about 15mm (½in) from the ends of half the strands in each end and then twist the remaining strands together to form a smooth join.

(7) Using a narrow lace braid

A narrow lace braid, made to the shape and size of the footside edge of the lace, may be attached to fabric and the lace then flat overcast to the braid. This is ideal where you wish to use one of the direct methods but may wish to remove the lace at a later date.

Any of the direct methods described above may be used, the main problem being that the narrow braid will not hold its shape well while you are positioning it. To overcome this, place the *main* piece of lace into position on the fabric and then pin and tack the braid into place inside the lace footside. Now remove the main piece of lace while the braid is stitched into place, the excess fabric cut away and any additional finishing (e.g. the neckline of a collar) is completed.

The lace may then be attached by flat overcasting its footside to the outer edge of the braid (see fig. 24). If the edge is very irregular the placing of the lace may be helped by laying in marker threads (which may be cut out later) on the braid as it is made. Fig. 23 shows a piece of lace being attached in this way.

fig. 22 *Detail of handkerchief illustrated in fig. 118. Right side shows lace attached by cording.*

fig 23 *Detail of collar shown in figs. 107 and 108. Wrong side shows narrow lace braid attached with three-sided stitch. Fabric and lace are tacked to paper before overcasting. Note marker threads on braid.*

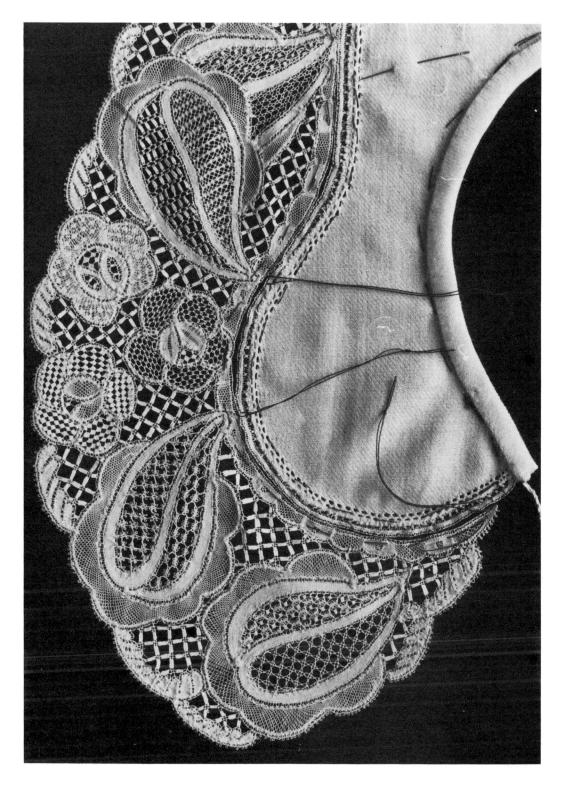

INDIRECT METHODS

Always make the fabric to fit the lace; it is very difficult to make the lace accurately fit a previously prepared piece of fabric.

In order to obtain the right size and shape of fabric, place the lace on the material with its straight edge parallel to the grain of the fabric and pin into place. If it is a circle or an irregular shape check that you have positioned it accurately (see page 19). Tack round, alongside the footside edge of the lace, and then remove the lace. This tacked line gives the size and shape required, and any allowances for hems or seams are added to it before cutting out.

When the fabric centre has been completed the lace is stitched in place with a flat overcasting stitch worked from the wrong side, as shown in fig. 24. Take up the minimum possible fabric at the very edge and only the footside edge pairs of the lace. To position the lace and fabric accurately it is often helpful to tack the fabric, face down, to a piece of paper or clean fabric. Now lay the lace in its correct position, face down, and tack it in place on the paper. It will then be firmly held while the overcasting is worked, taking care not to catch the paper into the stitching.

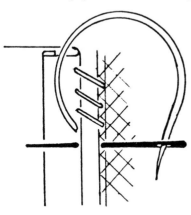

fig. 24   *Flat overcasting lace to a finished hem.*

When making a hem its depth should be in proportion to the finished size, that is, small items will need narrow hems and larger items will benefit from a deeper one.

(1) Double fold hem (figs. 25 and 29)

This gives an extremely strong, neat finish which will withstand much use, but it is not suitable for circles or curves. It may be used for any fabric and is ideal for those which fray easily or are likely to pull away from a stitched edge.

fig. 25   *Detail of handkerchief illustrated in fig. 117. Right side shows double fold hem pin-stitched in place. Actual size of lace 48mm ($1\frac{7}{8}$in.) square.*

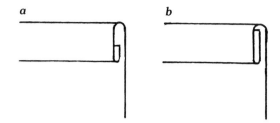

a   *b*

fig. 26 *a* *Double fold hem.* *b* *Double fold hem for sheer fabrics.*

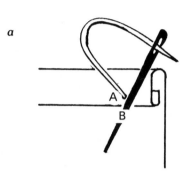

a   *b*

fig. 27 *Slip stitch hem.* *a* *Come out of fold at A. Pick up one thread at B.* *b* *Go back into fold at A and along fold to C. Do not pull stitches tightly.*

The hem is folded into place as shown in fig. 26a; on sheer fabrics (e.g. organdie) the raw edge must go right up into the fold (see fig. 26b). It is then stitched into place with an invisible slip stitch (see fig. 27), pin stitch (see fig. 19) or a drawn thread hem may be made (see page 58). On some fine fabrics the extra thickness of fabric in the hem will show from the right side, making it impossible for the completed hem to be invisible. In this case it is better to choose pin stitch which will make a decorative feature of the hem. Any corners should be mitred (see page 32).

(2) Single fold hem (fig. 52)
If a double hem is too bulky (particularly for a very narrow hem on a tiny piece) then a single fold hem may be made. This method is not suitable for curved shapes and any corners should be mitred (see page 32). Nor is it suitable for fabrics which fray badly.

The single fold is held in place by working through both layers, using three-sided stitch, four-sided stitch or two parallel rows of pin stitch. The excess fabric is then cut away close to the stitching (see fig. 28). Alternatively, buttonhole stitch (with the looped edge on the fold) could be worked over the folded edge. For a decorative hem, two or three rows of four-sided stitch may be worked close to the fold (see fig. 61).

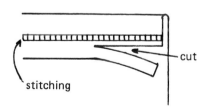

cut

stitching

fig. 28 *Single fold hem.*

31

To mitre a corner (fig. 29)

Having decided on the finished size of the fabric, either press a crease along this line or mark it with tacking stitches (see fig. 30a – broken line). Creasing will be the quickest method on fabrics which will hold a crease well, but tacking may be easier to follow and will have to be used on fabrics which will not hold a crease. Decide on the depth of the hem required, measure this amount out from the previously marked line and crease or tack to mark (see fig. 30a – dotted line).

Now lay the fabric out flat and cut round the edge about 6mm (¼in.) out from the second line you marked. (If the fabric is inclined to fray, leave a more generous margin and trim it just before turning under the hem; if it is sheer make this allowance the same depth as the hem).

Fold the fabric, right sides together, diagonally across the corner at an angle of *exactly* 45 degrees to the cut edge and line up the marked lines as in fig. 30b. Now back stitch, using tiny stitches, from A to B (see fig. 30b). This line *must* be at a 90 degree angle to the fold; the accuracy of the corner depends on it. If you are making a single fold hem, stitch right to the raw edge; for a double fold hem, stop at the outer marked line. Cut the excess fabric about 4mm (⅛in.) from the stitching as shown in fig. 30b.

Turn the point carefully to the right side, easing it out gently with a needle. Press the raw edge under, along the outer marked line and press the hem into its correct place, where it will be stitched by your chosen method.

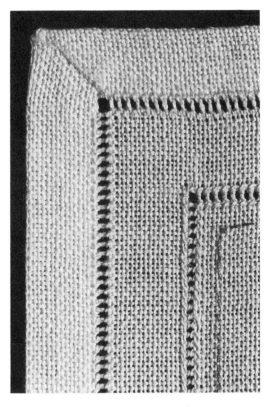

fig. 29 *Detail of place mat illustrated in fig. 119. Wrong side shows mitred corner on double fold hem and stitching to attach lace.*

fig. 30 *To mitre a corner:* **a** *Mark position of finished edge (broken line). Measure depth of hem and mark (dotted line).* **b** *Fold as shown. Stitch A to B. Cut 4mm (⅛in.) from stitching as shown.*

a

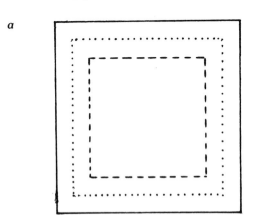

b

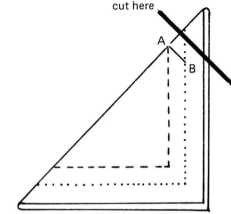

(3) Rolled hem (figs. 31 and 32)

This method gives a delicate, firm hem and is ideal for straight edges but is not easy to handle on tiny pieces. It can also be difficult to achieve a neat corner. If a rolled hem is to be worked across a seam it is usually easier to roll the hem first and then make the seam.

First work a line of small machine stitches about 4mm (⅛in.) *outside the required finished*

fig. 31 (below left)   *Detail of cuff frill illustrated in fig. 112. Right side shows rolled hem and join in lace (in line with seam).*

fig. 32   *Reverse of fig. 31 shows rolled hem. Note threads formed into four rolls at back of gimp where lace is joined. Actual width of lace 19mm (¾in.).*

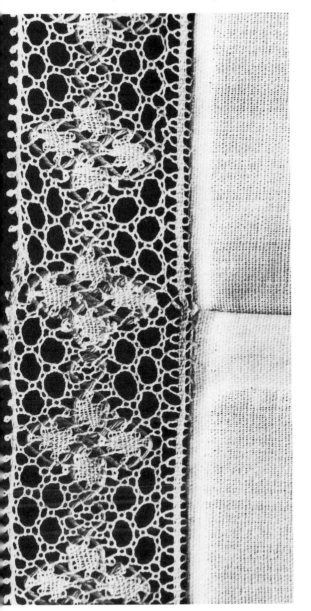

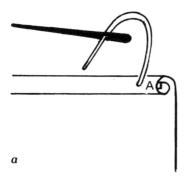

a

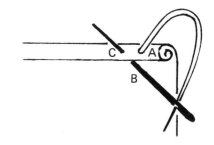

b

fig. 33 *Rolled hem. **a** Come out from roll at A. **b** Pick up one thread at B, slide needle under roll and come out at C ready for next stitch. Repeat **b** along roll, pulling thread up into place after every few stitches.*

fig. 34 (below) *Detail of mat illustrated in fig. 83. Reverse shows join in bias binding (near centre of picture). Actual width of lace 44mm (1¾in.).*

edge and then cut the fabric close to the stitching. This stitching will stabilise the edge and make rolling easier. Roll the edge between your first finger and thumb (it will help if they are moistened) and stitch into place as you roll. The working of the stitch is shown in fig. 33.

(4) Bias binding

When a circle or a curve is to be made from a fabric which tends to fray or pull away from stitching, it is necessary to use a bias binding. It is never easy to make tiny circles accurately by this method, although it gives a finish which will withstand much use and is ideal for larger items.

The binding may be a commercial one, but it is usually better to cut your own from the same fabric; you will then be sure that the binding will wash and wear in the same way and will be a perfect match. If the fabric is fairly bulky, use a bias strip cut from a lightweight fabric of the same fibre content (e.g. a fine, matching linen was used for the binding shown in fig. 34).

Cut out the required shape adding turnings (about 7mm (¼in.) to 10mm (⅜in.) is usually sufficient), and also a strip of binding of the required finished width plus turnings. If it is necessary to join the binding to obtain the required length, do so by stitching along the straight grain of the fabric as shown in fig. 35 and

then press the seam open. Pin the single layer to the fabric, right sides together and raw edges level. Stretch the bias binding slightly on outer curves and ease it slightly on inner curves so that when the binding is turned to the wrong side of the fabric it will lie flat (see fig. 36). Join the ends of the binding as shown in fig. 35.

The binding is now stitched into place just *outside* the required finished line. This may be done by machine, stretching both the fabric and binding slightly while working so that when finished the edge of the fabric will lie flat.

Clip the seam at intervals as shown in fig. 37 and then turn the bias over to the wrong side of the fabric, rolling the fold over so that no binding will show from the front. The raw edge of the

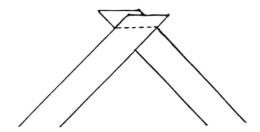

fig. 35   *Join bias binding by stitching along the straight grain of the fabric.*

fig. 36   *Pin bias binding into place, stretching it on round outer curves and easing it on inner curves.*

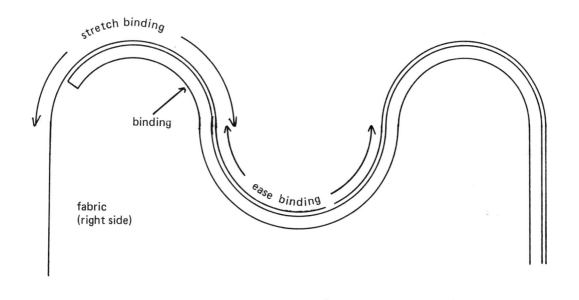

stretch binding

binding

ease binding

fabric
(right side)

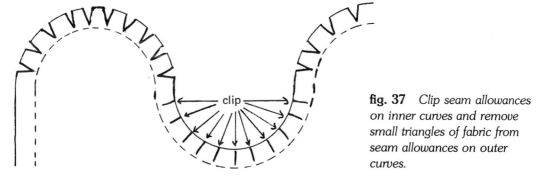

clip

fig. 37   *Clip seam allowances on inner curves and remove small triangles of fabric from seam allowances on outer curves.*

fig. 38 *Mat finished with a single layer bias binding. Actual size 184mm (7¼in.) across, including lace.*

fig. 39 (opposite, left) *Detail of fig. 38. Right side shows four sided stitch in straight and curved line.*

fig. 40 (opposite, far left) *Detail of fig. 38. Wrong side shows binding cut close to stitching and a join in binding. Actual width of lace 29mm (1⅛in.).*

binding may now be turned under, making sure that the finished binding is the same depth all round. It is then stitched into place with an invisible hem stitch or pin stitch. If pin stitch (or any other decorative stitch) is used, be particularly careful that the stitching is the same distance from the finished edge all the way round.

If turning the raw edge under is likely to be too bulky, the bias may be treated in exactly the same way as a single fold hem (see page 31). This is an ideal method for bindings which do not readily fray and where a very narrow binding is needed (see figs. 38, 39 and 40).

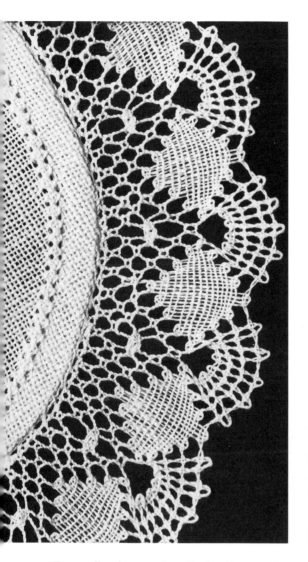

For smaller shapes, where the binding must be finished with a folded edge and the hem must be narrow, it is easier to use a folded binding, which must be cut from a lightweight fabric to avoid excessive bulk (see fig. 41).

To do this, cut a bias strip of fabric twice the required finished width plus two seam allowances. Fold and press the strip in half lengthwise (wrong sides together) and tack it into place on the right side of the fabric with all the raw edges even, as shown in fig. 42. To make the join, open out the binding, join as shown in fig. 35 and then refold the binding.

Now stitch through all three layers and then layer the seams to reduce bulk as shown in fig. 43 before clipping the seams as shown in fig. 37. Roll the binding over to the wrong side of the fabric and stitch into place with an invisible slip stitch or pin stitch. If the hem cannot be made invisible, it is better to use pin stitch.

A binding may also be used on geometric shapes such as hexagons. In this case it should be a straight binding, and when it is rolled over to the wrong side it must be folded neatly in the corners as shown in fig. 44.

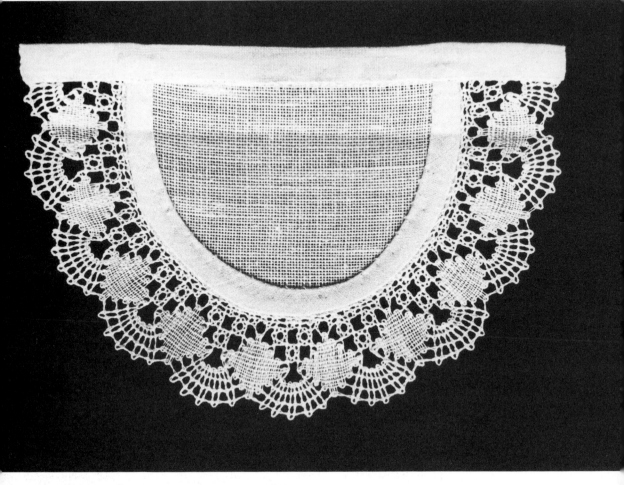

fig. 41 *Reverse of pocket flap illustrated in
fig. 111. Finished with a folded binding.
Actual width of lace 26mm (1in.).*

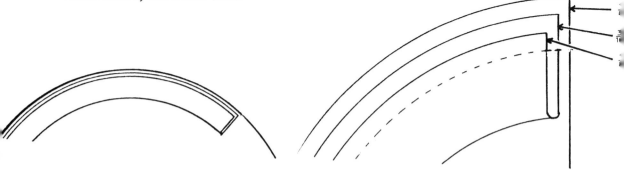

fig. 42 *Place double fold bias binding in
position shown.*

fig. 43 *Layer seam by cutting as shown.*

38

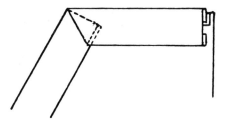

fig. 44 *Fold the binding neatly in the corners (the dotted line represents the fold hidden under the binding).*

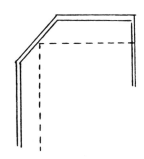

fig. 45 *Clip the fabric away from the corner, close to the stitching.*

(5) Double fabric

This method is ideal for small, irregular shapes where you do not wish to use the direct methods but bias binding would be difficult to handle. It would be wasteful of fabric to use it for larger pieces.

Place the two layers of fabric together, right sides facing, and mark out the shape required. (The backing fabric could be different if required, e.g. a lighter weight). Stitch round the shape by hand or machine, through both layers, leaving a small opening through which the shape may later be turned. Layer and clip the seams (see figs. 43 and 37) and clip the corners of rectangles or squares as shown in fig. 45.

Turn the shape through to the right side and press it flat. The opening is then closed with ladder stitch (see fig. 46). You may now proceed in one of three ways:

(a) If the fabric will stay perfectly flat just by pressing, the lace may be overcast into place in the usual way.

(b) Work a row of pin stitch, three-sided stitch or four-sided stitch through both layers of fabric a little way in, to hold them firmly together and give a decorative effect (see fig. 89). For both of these methods it is advisable to use a very light-weight fabric to avoid a bulky finish.

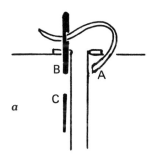

fig. 46 *Ladder stitch.* **a** *Come out of fold at A. Go through opposite fold B–C.*

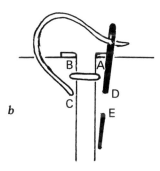

b Go through opposite fold D–E. Repeat a and b several times, then pull thread firmly to close opening.

fig. 47 (above) *Double fabric method held flat with four-sided stitch. Actual width of lace 13mm (½in.). (Pricking appears in* Making Lace with Little Grey Rabbit *by Dorothy Cox).*

fig. 48 (above, right) *Reverse of fig. 47 shows the back layer of fabric cut away.*

(c) If the above method results in too bulky an effect for your purpose, the back layer of fabric may be cut away carefully, close to the stitching. The resultant finish is a shaped facing which has been stitched into place (see figs. 47 and 48). If the fabric is to be cut away, a stronger finish will be achieved if three-sided or four-sided stitch is used.

(6) Buttonhole stitch (fig. 79)

The direct use of buttonhole stitch has been described on page 19 but there are occasions (e.g. when the lace may need to be removed) where it may be preferable to use it indirectly.

To do this, mark out the required shape (see page 30) with small running stitches just inside the required finished edge. Work buttonhole stitch round the shape, just covering the running stitches and with the loops on the edge which is to be cut away. When the buttonholing is complete, cut away the excess fabric using a sharp pair of scissors, as close to the stitching as possible. The lace is then attached by overcasting it to the looped edge of the stitches; in this case it is easier to work from the right side, taking care that your stitching is very neat.

This is an ideal method for achieving small,

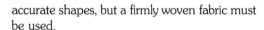

accurate shapes, but a firmly woven fabric must be used.

ATTACHING LACE TO NET (FIGS. 49, 50 AND 51)

This fabric presents its own difficulties because of the open nature of its construction and the ease with which it can be pulled out of shape. It does not usually fray easily and hemming would spoil its appearance, thus making a direct method the best choice. Most of these can appear rather heavy, but pin stitch gives a firm and pleasing result and buttonhole stitch works well when the thread used is very fine and only one stitch is made in each mesh of the net.

An alternative method would be to work back stitch as described on page 50 and then to cut the

fig. 49 (above, left)   *Lace attached to net with buttonhole stitch. Actual width of lace 35mm (1⅜in.).*

fig. 50 (above)   *Lace attached to net with pin stitch. Actual width of lace 45mm (1¾in.).*

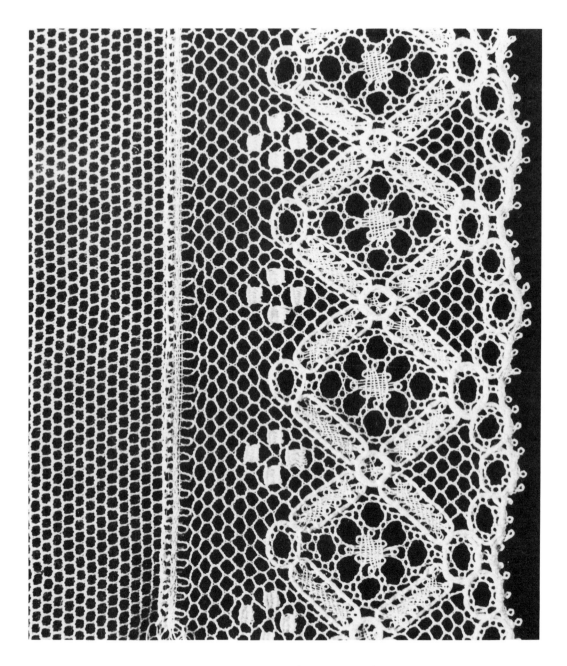

excess net away from the back of the lace. Whichever method is used, great care must be taken with the tension of the stitches to avoid puckering. Tack both the net and lace to stiff, coloured paper to hold them in shape whilst stitching, taking care not to include the paper in the stitches.

fig. 51 *Lace attached to net with back stitch. Actual width of lace 42mm (1⅝in.).*

CHAPTER FOUR

Using Lace Insertions

Lace for insertion usually takes one of three forms:

(1) Straight strips with the ends either enclosed in a seam (e.g. for the front of a blouse) or joined into a tube (e.g. for the hem of a skirt or pillow case).
(2) Small motifs.
(3) Closed borders with corners (e.g. for a tablecloth).

Each of these situations needs considering separately; if there is also to be a lace edging, try to choose a similar method for both the edging and insertion.

(1) STRAIGHT STRIPS

Any of the direct methods (on pages 19 to 28) could be used, but if the strip of lace is narrow it may be difficult to cut the fabric away from the back of the lace without damage. A double or single fold hem, indirect buttonhole stitch or a rolled hem (see pages 30, 31, 33 and 40) would all be easier to handle, the choice depending on the weight of the lace and fabric and its intended use. If a curved insertion is being used, a bias binding could be chosen, selecting the most suitable method of finishing it (see page 34).

If the strip is to be joined into a 'tube', join the lace on the pillow and make the seam in the fabric before hemming it ready for attaching the lace (although a rolled hem is best made before making the seam).

(2) SMALL MOTIFS

Remember that motifs for insertion need a footside edge, not a purl edge. Most prickings can easily be worked in this way.

Some of the direct methods (pages 19 to 25) may be used and, although for small, awkward shapes they appear to be the best choice, it can be difficult to remove the fabric from the back without damage to the lace (see fig. 52). The easiest method in this case is to use buttonhole stitch indirectly (see page 40 and fig. 79). If a finished hem is required round these motifs a facing, which can be any shape, may be made as follows.

Cut a piece of the facing material larger than the lace and place it on the fabric, right sides together. Stitch round the required shape through both layers, working with the fabric uppermost to follow the grain. Then cut away the fabric and facing from the centre, leaving small seams which should be layered and clipped where required, especially in any corners (see figs. 37, 43 and 53).

Turn the facing through to the wrong side where it may now be treated in the same way as a single or double fold hem. If a double fold hem is used, the seam allowances should be mitred on any corners in the same way as for a single fold hem (see page 32 and figs. 54 and 55).

Curved shapes may be finished with a bias binding (see page 34), remembering that it should be eased on round inner curves. This is satisfactory for larger motifs but a very small accurate shape is difficult to achieve.

fig. 52 *Detail of handkerchief illustrated in fig. 117. Motif (actual diameter 39mm (1½in.)) inserted using three-sided stitch. Single fold hem finished with three-sided stitch.*

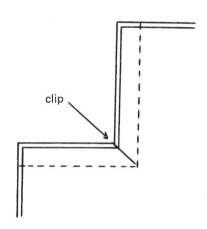

fig. 53 *Clip the seam allowance in the corner, to almost reach the stitching.*

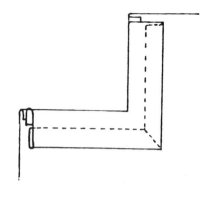

fig. 54 *The broken line indicates the position of the mitred seam allowance under the facing.*

44

fig. 55 *Detail of cushion illustrated in fig. 120. Reverse shows corner of centre motif and facing. Note join in lace.*

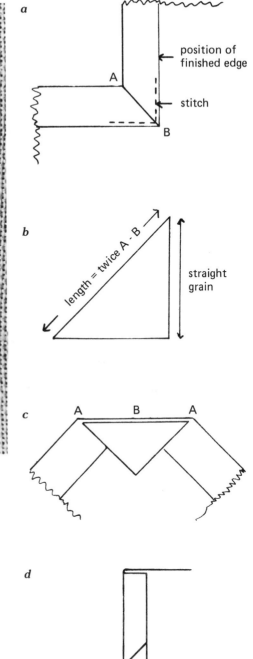

fig. 56 *a Stitch as shown and cut A–B. b Cut a triangle of fabric as shown. c Stitch triangle to slit A–B–A. d Turn hem and triangle to wrong side of fabric and stitch hem.*

fig. 57 *Detail of handkerchief illustrated in fig. 117. Reverse shows added triangle of fabric on inner corner. Note lace was started with two cloth stitch diamonds.*

(3) CLOSED BORDERS WITH CORNERS

Any of the direct methods on pages 19 to 25 may be used in this situation if the fabric and its intended use permit, remembering that it may be difficult to cut the fabric away behind the lace. None of these methods presents any problem at the corners but most of the indirect methods do (with the exception of buttonhole stitch).

The fabric which is to be attached to the inner edge of the lace may have an ordinary double or single fold hem with mitred corners (see pages 30 and 31).

The corners to accommodate the outer edge of the lace, however, need a different treatment, there being a choice of two methods.

Method (1)

Reinforce the corner by machining along the required finished line as shown in fig. 56a, using a small stitch. Cut the fabric right up into the corner along the line A–B (fig. 56a) and also cut a small triangle of the fabric as shown in fig. 56b.

Now open out the slit so that A–B–A forms a straight line and pin the triangle to the slit (right sides facing) as shown in fig. 56c. Using a small stitch, machine stitch the triangle into place along A–B–A as close to the edge as possible. The triangle and hem may now be turned to the wrong side of the fabric (see fig. 56d), where the hem is finished by the chosen method (and to match the inner edge). If a double fold hem is used, mitre the seam allowances at the outer corners as for a single fold hem (see figs. 54 and 57 and page 32).

This method is not suitable for bulky fabrics nor those which fray easily. In these cases use method (2), which is suitable for most fabrics.

Method (2)

Cut four strips of straight binding (either the same fabric or a lighter weight one) to the dimensions shown in fig. 58a, remembering to

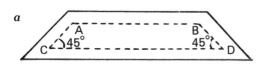

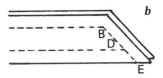

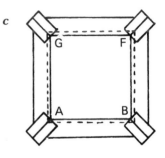

fig. 58 *a A–B = Required finished length of edge. C–D = A–B plus twice depth of hem. Distance between line A–B and C–D = Depth of hem. Angles BDC and ACD each equal 45 degrees.* **b** *Join two strips along B–D–E.* **c** *Join remaining strips, press seams open, place on fabric and stitch A–B–F–G–A.*

add turnings all round (about 7mm (¼in.) is usually sufficient).

Place two strips together, right sides facing, and stitch them together along B–D–E as shown in fig. 58b, then press the seam open as in fig. 58c. Prepare the other three corners of the binding in the same way and then place it on the fabric, right sides together. Stitch all round along A–B–F–G–A (see fig. 58c), clip the turnings right into the corners and turn the binding to the wrong side. It may now be treated as a double or

fig. 59 *Detail of cushion illustrated in fig. 120. Reverse shows corner of border insertion. Note seam across corner of binding.*

single fold hem (see pages 30 and 31), finishing the corners as in Method 1 (see figs. 54 and 59).

This method could be adapted for other shapes by altering the angle at which the strips are joined.

CHAPTER FIVE

Methods of Applying Lace

For items which are to receive a great deal of use and laundering, it is often better to apply the lace over the fabric. This will take a great deal of strain off the lace and will help to retain its shape with the minimum effort during laundering.

When lace (especially motifs) is applied to material it is important that it should appear as an integral part of the design and not just stuck on as an afterthought. This problem can often be overcome by an outlining row of pin stitch, drawn thread work or other decorative stitchery (see place mat in fig. 60). Take care also that the texture of the fabric does not overpower the lace.

If the back of the material is to be covered in some way, the ends of the lace may be darned through to the back and left. When the lace does not have a definite right side it is often easier to place it face down on the fabric (i.e. the way it was worked). Each knotted pair is then easily accessible to be threaded into a needle, both ends together, and taken through to the back. Unless the fabric is very tightly woven it is possible to pull the knot gently through to the back, taking care not to distort the lace.

Ends which have been darned to the back may be covered with an iron-on interfacing or they may be enclosed between two layers of fabric

fig. 60 *Detail of place mat illustrated in fig. 119. The lace has been applied invisibly with back stitch and then surrounded by a line of drawn thread hem stitch. Fig. 29 shows a detail of the reverse.*

which are bonded together with an iron-on hemming web, but only if the material will withstand the heat and steam which may be required. Either of these methods of covering the ends will thicken the work, which may be satisfactory for a bookmark but will not be acceptable when a motif is applied to the corner of a handkerchief or a garment of lightweight fabric.

If the back of the material is not to be covered in some way, these ends must be dealt with by darning them into the lace before it is applied. It is also advisable to do this if the lace is to be applied to a lightweight fabric where the ends could show through to the right side.

The lace can be stitched to the fabric invisibly or by using pin stitch or some other decorative stitch (e.g. three-sided or four-sided stitch). Invisible stitching would be ideal for applying lace to an article where the reverse will not be seen in use (see figs. 98 and 101), but pin stitch will withstand more wear and be neater on the reverse where this is important (see fig. 61). It may however be difficult to remove the lace without damage at a later date. Take care to work this stitching far enough from the motif for the decorative holes to show.

For invisible stitching, use the lace thread but if pin stitch is employed to stitch down a contrasting lace, use a thread to match the *fabric*, placing the stitches as shown in fig. 19g.

The lace is stitched down invisibly by using a small running stitch or back stitch (see fig. 62); back stitch will prevent the thread from being accidentally pulled. In either case make only a tiny stitch on the right side of the work, avoiding if possible making them over the edge of the lace where they may show. They will be less noticeable if they are just inside the edge; fig. 63 shows some suggested positions for these stitches. Their spacing will depend upon the intended use of the lace; if it is to be placed in a frame they may be widely spaced but if it is to be subject to wear they should be very close to each other. Take care that the back is very neat if it is to be exposed, and that there are no long threads carried across between stitches. Also check that they are not

fig. 61 *Detail of handkerchief illustrated in fig. 117. Motif (actual diameter 39mm (1½in.)) applied using pin stitch and single fold hem finished with two rows of four-sided stitch.*

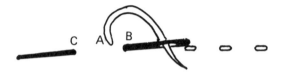

fig. 62 *Back stitch. Come up at A, go in at B to make a tiny stitch on the front. Come up at C to make a long stitch on the back.*

50

pulled too tight, thus pulling the lace down into the fabric instead of allowing it to lie on top. This is particularly important when using pile fabrics.

fig. 63 *Suggested positions of stitches to apply lace invisibly.* ***a*** *Torchon type edge.* ***b*** *Beds/Maltese and Bucks Point type edge.* ***c*** *Honiton type edge, with and without purls.* ***d*** *Beds/Maltese type, plaited edge.* ***e*** *Cloth stitch.*

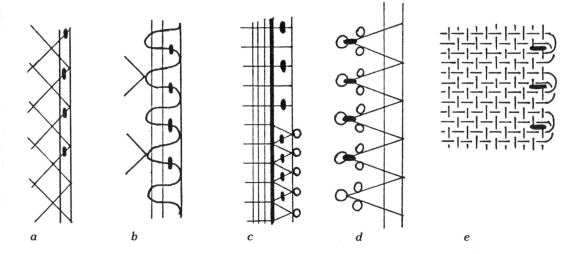

a   *b*   *c*   *d*   *e*

CHAPTER SIX

Combining Lace with Embroidery

Many embroidery techniques may be combined with lace. Drawn thread work and cutwork are undoubtedly ancestors of needle-made laces and these techniques can combine well with bobbin laces, especially the coarser ones. Carrickmacross lace is in fact a type of embroidery (appliqué on net) as is Limerick lace (darning on net), and both would combine well with a fine lace edging. Shadow work has a delicacy which looks well with lace and blackwork may have a 'lacey' appearance which will enhance a lace edging. Cathedral window patchwork is a good vehicle for mounting small lace motifs and making them look important.

More than one embroidery technique may be used at a time. For instance, shapes outlined in shadow work could contain pulled thread work fillings, or drawn thread and pulled thread work could be combined to complement your lace. Do be careful, however, to avoid a 'bitty' appearance. When combined with lace, embroidery is best kept fairly simple so that it will not overpower the lace. Remember always that the finished item should appear incomplete if either the embroidery or the lace were to be removed.

Although some completed articles (using only a few techniques) are described, it is hoped that these will serve as jumping-off points for your own ideas. Remember that the most effective ideas are likely to be those which echo your lace in some way.

Having chosen the design for your embroidery it must now be transferred to the fabric. There are a number of ways of doing this, but one of the simplest and most accurate is to use tissue paper.

Trace the design onto tissue paper, using ink which will not smudge (avoid pencil; it can rub off onto your fabric and is almost impossible to remove). Draw lines across the centres (across length and width) of the design and mark the centres of the fabric with tacking stitches, following the straight grain exactly. Use these lines to position the design accurately on the fabric and pin into place, keeping the paper smooth. Now tack through tissue and material, following the design lines, using a fairly large stitch for bold shapes and small ones for intricate lines. The paper may then be carefully removed, this being easier to do if the point of a needle is first run around the design lines.

If the fabric is sheer a different method may be used. Place the fabric over your design and draw it onto the material using a water washable embroidery marker (from haberdashers). The drawing may also be removed with damp cotton wool if required.

Many embroidery techniques are easier to work in a frame as a more even tension may be maintained, and puckering of the finished piece avoided. There is the additional advantage that you may stand back from your work to assess its appearance.

There are a number of types of frame available. Small round tambour frames have always been popular because they are quick to use, but they do suffer from disadvantages. They are likely to cause marking and creasing of the fabric; areas already worked are likely to be crushed; and the embroidery will need to be removed from the frame to assess the overall effect. They are ideal for tiny pieces of work.

Rotating and slate frames overcome these problems, rotating frames being less expensive. They are available in a variety of roller lengths and it is probably better to buy the longest you can afford; small pieces may still be worked in it. Each roller will have a piece of webbing fastened to it; it will save time if you find the exact centre of each roller and mark the webbing permanently at this point.

To frame the fabric, find the centre of the fabric and line it up with the centre of the roller. Make a single fold on the edge of the fabric and then, starting at the centre of the roller, overcast this folded edge to the edge of the webbing with strong easily visible stitches (to assist in removing them later), stretching the fabric as you go. When this is completed, attach the opposite end of the fabric to the other roller in the same way.

Now insert the roller into the side arms and tighten the screws to fasten one roller firmly in place. Roll any excess fabric onto the other roller and then pull the fabric tight across the frame before tightening the screws to hold this roller firmly in place. As work progresses the fabric may be released from one roller and taken up on the other.

Finally, lace through the edges of the fabric, as shown in fig. 64, round the side arms of the frame to tighten the fabric (this makes a world of difference when using the frame and is well worth the effort). If the fabric is inclined to fray, turn under a single hem which may be reinforced by inserting a string or cord into the fold and lacing over it.

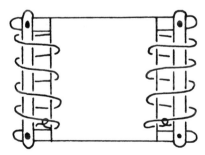

fig. 64 *Lace over side arms of frame to stretch fabric evenly.*

When working in a frame each stitch is made with at least two movements, working up and down. Practice working with your 'best' hand under the frame and your other hand on top. With practice you will be able to work much more quickly.

DRAWN THREAD WORK

A double fold hem (see page 30) is often attractive when finished with a drawn thread hem stitch but more elaborate work also combines well with lace. Torchon is especially suitable because both techniques produce very geometric designs; in this case it is advisable to work samples so that you may choose those designs which will best combine with and echo the lace.

The basis of the technique is that selected threads are withdrawn from the fabric which is then both decorated and strengthened by the stitchery. There are many ways of decorating the drawn threads; only those used in the traycloth illustrated in figs. 65 and 66 are described in detail here. This technique should not be confused with pulled work where no threads are removed, the pattern being achieved by pulling the threads of the fabric tightly together with the stitches.

If the embroidery design requires threads to be withdrawn in both directions, then an evenweave fabric must be used. It is available in cotton or linen from specialist embroidery suppliers and is sold with a given number of threads to the inch, those in warp and weft being equal. These fabrics fray easily, making it worthwhile to neaten the edges with a zig-zag or overcasting stitch before commencing work. A limited range of colours is available, the most pleasing results being obtained when fabric and lace match exactly.

A simple drawn thread hem, where only one thread is to be withdrawn, may be worked on any fabric which appears even and from which the thread can be easily withdrawn. The same is also true if the drawn thread work is to form bands across the fabric in one direction only.

The thread used for the stitching should be

fairly soft, the same thickness as those of the fabric or slightly finer, and match exactly. It is usually possible to use the same thread as that used for the lace. On the completed piece of work the stitches should be inconspicuous, the pattern being created by the spaces.

A blunt needle should be used for the stitching to prevent it from splitting the threads of the fabric; a No. 24 tapestry needle usually proves suitable.

Once a thread has been cut and withdrawn it cannot easily be replaced so, to avoid wasting expensive fabric, it is as well to plan very carefully before starting work. It is often helpful to mark with tacking the areas to be worked and if this is done as a counted stitch (e.g. under four threads, over the next four) it will then be much easier to

fig. 65 *Traycloth combining drawn thread work and torchon lace. Actual size, including lace, 585mm × 439mm (23in. × 17¼in.).*

fig. 66 *Detail of fig. 65. Wrong side. The lace was joined just to the right of corner.*

count the fabric threads to check that there are the correct number for the required design.

For a first piece of drawn thread work it is easier to work bands of embroidery where the ends may be enclosed in a seam rather than to try working around a square, because the number of threads needed for the pattern does not have to be worked out in advance (see page 89).

Withdrawing threads

To withdraw a thread, lift the centre of it with a needle and cut. Then withdraw it, in each direction, a little at a time as far as required. If the band of embroidery does not extend to the edges of the fabric then these withdrawn threads must be finished off as follows: each end is threaded into a needle and darned back into the remaining fabric, on the wrong side, for about 7mm ($\frac{1}{4}$in.) as shown in fig. 67. Take care not to pull the fabric out of shape. The ends of the thread can then be cut off close to the fabric. If several threads are removed, this edge can be strengthened by working overcasting or buttonhole stitch over it.

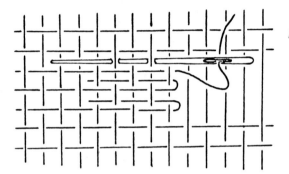

fig. 67   *Darn the cut ends into the fabric.*

Hemstitching

To make a simple ladder effect, withdraw two threads from the fabric and then hem stitch along one edge of the drawn area as shown in fig. 68, taking the threads together in groups of two. To start, darn the thread into the fabric and then work the hem stitch over this darned end, holding it firmly in place.

Now work another row of hem stitch along the other edge, working over the same groups of two threads (see fig. 69). The size of the 'ladder' can be altered by withdrawing more threads before stitching and more threads could be included in each bunch. If this method is to be used as an outline to a design it is very effective if only one thread is withdrawn.

a

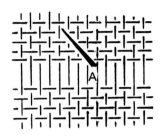

b

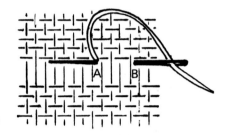

c

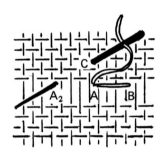

d

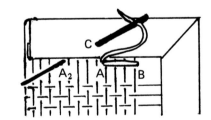

fig. 68   *Hem stitch: a Come out at A. b Go in at B and out again at A. Pull the sewing thread firmly to bunch the fabric threads.   c Go in at C and come out at A2. Repeat b and c along the row.   d Shows the position of the stitches when working a double fold hem. This stitch may also be worked from left to right.*

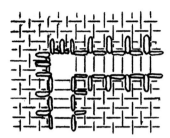

fig. 69 *Bunch the threads in groups of two on both edges of the drawn area to create a 'ladder'.*

A zig-zag effect is achieved in a similar way. Start by withdrawing four threads and work hem stitch along one edge, taking the threads into bunches of four. Now work along the other edge in the same way but making the bunches of four threads with two each from adjacent bunches of the first row (see fig. 70). Again, these bands could be varied by altering the number of withdrawn threads and those in each bunch.

Several of these bands of varying width may be used to create a richer effect. When these bands are separated by only four remaining threads, as in the traycloth, it is better to use double hem stitch over these threads (see fig. 71), bunching the threads as required for the effect you wish to achieve.

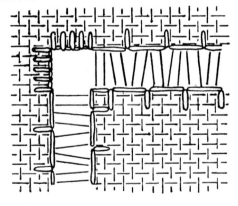

fig. 70 *Group threads in bunches of four. On opposite edge of drawn area bunch in groups of four, two each from adjacent bunches to create a zig-zag.*

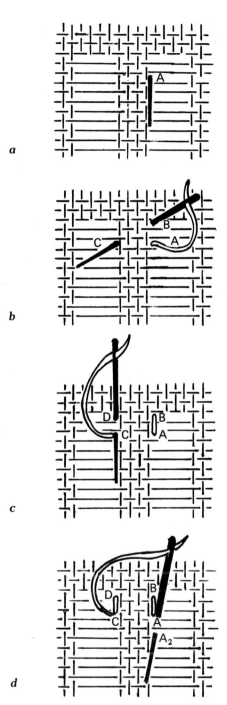

a

b

c

d

fig. 71 *Double hem stitch.* **a** *Come out at A.* **b** *Go in at B and out at C.* **c** *Go in at D and out again at C.* **d** *Go in at A and out again at A2. Repeat steps* **b**, **c** *and* **d**.

Interlacing

Interlaced bands are worked as follows: hem stitch both sides of the drawn area, taking the threads together in groups of two to form 'ladders'. They are then interlaced as shown in fig. 72, taking care that the interlacing thread, which may be thicker than that used for the rest of the embroidery, lies flat and does not pucker the work. These bands need to be fairly wide so that the work will lie flat when the interlacing is complete; a wide variety of multiple interlacing patterns is possible.

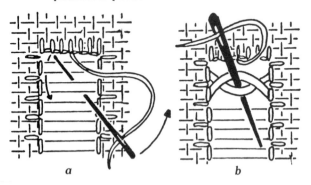

a   *b*

fig. 72 *Interlacing. Insert needle between two bars as shown in **a** and turn as indicated by arrows so that work appears as in **b**.*

To make a drawn thread hem

When these hems are made on squares or rectangles they need careful planning, especially when the finished piece must exactly fit a piece of lace.

First decide on the finished size of the fabric and mark it with pins. Now measure the required depth of hem in from this line and mark it with a line of counted tacking stitch (see fig. 73).

The threads immediately inside this line will be withdrawn as shown in fig. 73 but before withdrawing any threads check that when the required number have been withdrawn there will be the correct number left between A and B (see fig. 73) for the pattern you intend to work. You may need to slightly alter the hem depth (without altering the finished size) to achieve this. Check that the hem is still the same depth all round. The threads are then drawn and darned back as described on page 56. In the corners, where the threads have been removed in both directions,

fig. 73 *Preparing a drawn thread hem. Mark required size with pins. Mark depth of hem inside this line with counted tacking. Withdraw threads inside tacked line. Check number of threads between A and B is correct before withdrawing threads.*

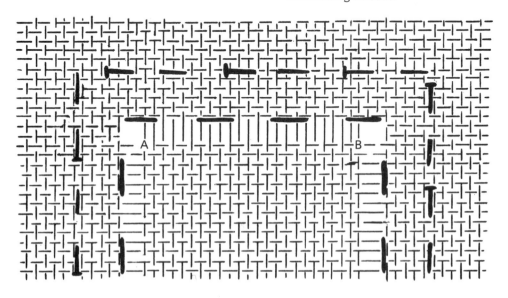

holes will appear. These will be dealt with later.

The counted tacking may now be removed and the required finished size, which was marked with pins, may now be marked by tacking or withdrawing one thread all round (withdrawing a thread helps to make a crisp fold).

Prepare and mitre the corners as described on page 32 and then turn them carefully. Tack the hem into place alongside the space left by the drawn threads. Starting at the corner, hem stitch the folded edge of the hem in place as shown in fig. 68d and bunching the threads as required for your chosen design. At the holes in the corners, the edge of the hole and the fold of the hem are held together either by overcasting or buttonhole stitch. The band (or bands) of embroidery is then completed as required.

If the holes formed in the corners are small they may be left as they are, but if they are large they will need to be strengthened in some way.

On the traycloth this was done by making needle woven bars over the remaining threads as shown in fig. 74. Take great care with the tension of these bars; their edges should be straight and even. Firstly work all the horizontal bars and then work the vertical ones. Some or all of these squares may be further embellished with loop stitch, which is worked at the same time as the

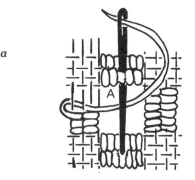

a

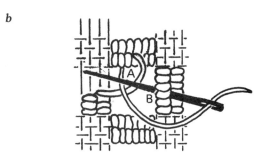

b

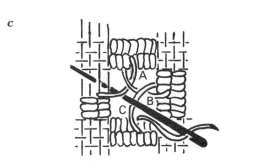

c

fig. 75 *Loop stitch.* ***a*** *Work half of needle woven bar. Make one buttonhole stitch at A.* ***b*** *Make one buttonhole stitch at B.* ***c*** *Make one buttonhole stitch at C. Continue making needle woven bar.*

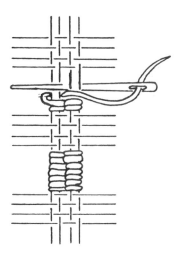

fig. 74 *Needle woven bars.*

vertical bars. Work half the bar, make the loop stitch as shown in fig. 75 and then complete the bar. The square motifs in the corners of the traycloth were worked in the same way, having buttonholed all round the square to neaten and strengthen it after withdrawing the threads.

If an area of any size is to be worked in this way it will help to keep the tension even if the fabric is tacked to a piece of stiff card of a contrasting colour before weaving the bars.

fig. 76 *Pricking for lace illustrated in fig. 65.*

The traycloth illustrated was worked on Glenshee evenweave linen with approximately 29 threads to the inch using Campbell's linen thread No. 60, which was also used for the lace. The pricking is shown in fig. 76 and requires 31 pairs of bobbins.

The finished work measures approximately 584mm × 438mm (23in. × 17¼in.) and fig. 77 shows the placing of the drawn areas. The embroidery was worked as follows: decide on the finished size and hem depth and then withdraw four threads all round for the single zig-zag band. The double zig-zag band is then prepared by removing four threads, leaving four (work over these in double hem stitch) and removing four more. When these bands are complete prepare the square motifs for needle weaving by alternately removing four threads and leaving four across the required width in both directions, and then withdraw a single thread all round the square to outline it.

The interlaced bands are prepared by withdrawing six threads, leaving four and withdrawing the next six. The outline to these bands and the inner edge of the design are all prepared by withdrawing one thread where indicated.

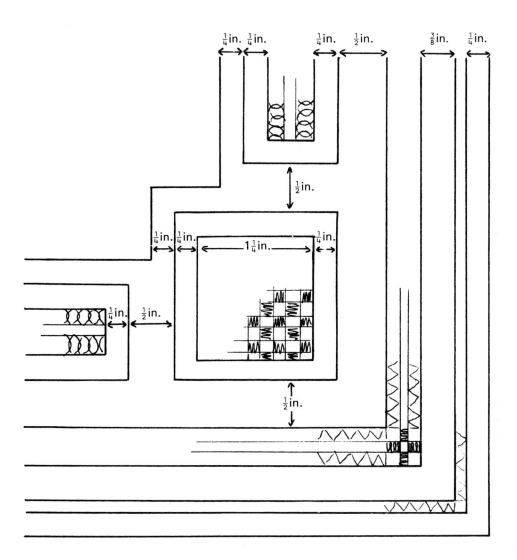

fig. 77 *Plan showing position of drawn areas on the traycloth.*

CUTWORK

Simple cutwork can be very effectively combined with lace, especially when it is attached to the fabric with buttonhole stitch, either directly or indirectly (see pages 19 and 40). For a more elaborate effect than that illustrated in figs. 78 and 79 larger areas of fabric may be cut away and the spaces enriched with bars and picots (instructions for working picots are not included).

Designs for cutwork are composed of two closely spaced lines which outline the spaces to be cut away.

The fabric used should be firmly woven so that the stitching will not pull away from the cut edges. The thread used may either match exactly or be in a contrasting colour, although the cut areas will be shown to advantage when using a matching thread.

The design is transferred to the fabric by tacking through tissue paper, just inside the design lines. These stitches should be kept small and the thread used be the same as that for the embroidery; they are left in place to reinforce and pad the edge.

When the position for a bar is reached, make a tiny back stitch inside the design line to anchor the thread, which is then taken over the fabric to the opposite outline where it is anchored in the same way (see fig. 80a). Make sure that the thread lies perfectly flat and does not pull the fabric. The thread is then brought back to the start of the bar in the same way and is again

fig. 78   Pocket flap which combines lace with simple cutwork.

fig. 79   Detail of fig. 78.

anchored before the running stitch is continued round the design to the next bar (see fig. 80b).

Buttonhole stitch is then worked over the design lines, covering all the tacking threads. The stitches should lie close enough to each other to cover the fabric without being crowded. The looped edge should face the areas to be cut away and the stitches are angled round the scallops as shown in fig. 81. Each stitch should be exactly the same length as its neighbour unless the width of the design line is being increased, in which case this gradation should be very smooth with each stitch being imperceptibly longer than its

62

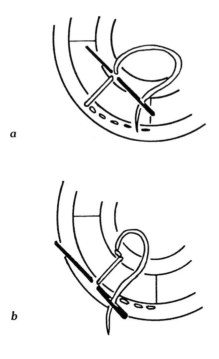

a

b

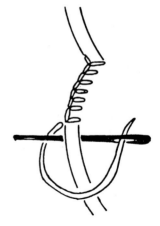

fig. 81 *On scallops, angle stitches as shown, making them touch each other.*

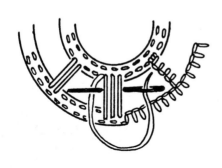

c

fig. 80 *a Work running stitch as far as bar. Anchor thread and then anchor it at opposite end of bar. **b** Bring thread back to start of bar, anchor it and continue in running stitch. **c** Work buttonhole stitch as far as bar. Anchor thread and take it to opposite end of bar. Work back in buttonhole stitch. Buttonhole stitches and threads in bars are shown spaced for clarity, but should touch each other.*

neighbour. Fasten the thread to start the buttonhole stitching by making a few running stitches between the design lines where they will be covered by the stitches. Finish by darning the thread into the back of the stitches.

When a bar is reached on this journey, the thread is again anchored before taking it across to the opposite side. The return journey is made by buttonhole stitching over the three laid threads (fig. 80c). Take care that the tension is even and the fabric is not caught with these stitches. You may find it easier to use a blunt needle or the eye of the needle to work these bars. At the end of the bar, anchor the thread inside the design line and then continue buttonholing round the design covering the end of the bar. Do not join in a new thread while working a bar, and when there are several bars make sure that the looped edge lies on the same side of each one.

After the stitching is complete, the areas of fabric to be removed are cut carefully away with a small sharp pair of pointed scissors, cutting as close to the looped edge of the stitches as possible. Take care not to cut the stitches, being particularly careful when cutting the fabric from behind the bars.

The design and pricing for the pocket flap illustrated are shown in fig. 82. Mark the exact position and shape of the finished lace and treat this as part of the embroidery. The lace was overcast into place after cutting away the fabric (see page 40).

The embroidery was worked with a single strand of stranded embroidery cotton on a linen fabric. The lace was made in D.M.C. Brilliante D'Alsace No. 30, using a total of 26 pairs of bobbins (there were four pairs of passives in the outer trail and three pairs in each of the other trails). The straight edge of the flap may be finished with a narrow hem; it will not be seen when it is folded back and stitched inside the pocket.

This flap could be used on a skirt, blouse or jacket pocket and two could be used to trim a plain V-neckline of a blouse or dress. In this case the shape could be modified by lengthening the straight edge to suit the neckline. This design could also be used to trim the ends of a wide tie.

BLACKWORK

This is a monochrome technique which traditionally was worked in black, with possibly a red or gold outline, on a white or cream fabric. It is equally attractive in other colours (but still keeping to one colour for any single piece of work). The overall effect is best if the lace is in the same colour as the embroidery.

Blue embroidery is very successful, but the mat illustrated was worked in a deep coral pink. White or pastel shades could be used on a dark ground, although it can be difficult to see the separate threads in order to count them. The colour of the thread chosen for the embroidery and lace must be strong enough to show up against the fabric when only a single strand is being used, but not so dark that the lace appears too heavy.

The fabric chosen must be an evenweave because the fillings are worked over counted threads. If you cannot find the colour of fabric

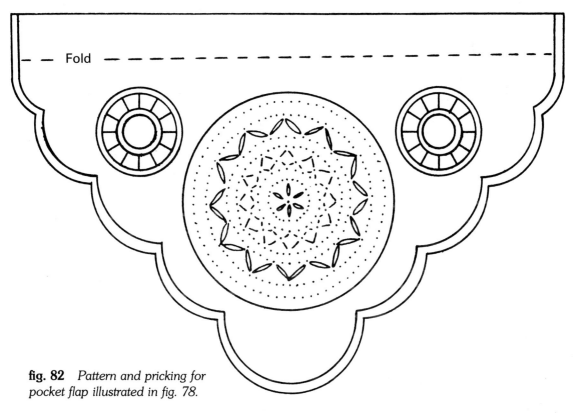

fig. 82 *Pattern and pricking for pocket flap illustrated in fig. 78.*

you require (and there is a limited range avail-able) consider dyeing the fabric. A blunt needle will be required for working the fillings and a sharp one for the outlines.

To be really effective, blackwork needs some pale areas and others which are very much darker. This can be done by filling some shapes with very light fillings and others with much heavier ones. Alternatively, the tone can be varied within one shape. This can be seen in the mat in figs. 83 and 84 where the fillings are darker towards the centre of the mat and

fig. 83 *Circular mat combining blackwork with torchon lace. Actual size, including lace 299mm (11¾in.) diameter.*

fig. 84 (opposite)   *Detail of fig. 83 to show the embroidery.*

become paler towards the outer edges. This variation in shade is *not* achieved with different shades of thread but in one of the following two ways, both of which were used in the mat illustrated:

(a) The same filling is used for the whole area, but is worked in different thicknesses of thread.

(b) The same thread is used for the entire area, the shading being achieved by leaving out elements of the filling to achieve a lighter result.

The fillings are worked in back stitch with possibly some cross stitches; if cross stitch is used, make sure that the top of each stitch slants in the same direction throughout the work. These fillings may be either fairly large and formal patterns, or smaller overall designs for a more textured effect. A tremendous variety is possible and it is well worth trying out ideas of your own, always remembering that they should be in the correct scale for your lace. Do try out samples before starting work; it is very difficult to remove stitches and leave the fabric looking untouched

fig. 85 *Pricking for lace illustrated in figs. 83 and 34. Fifteen complete heads make a circle.*

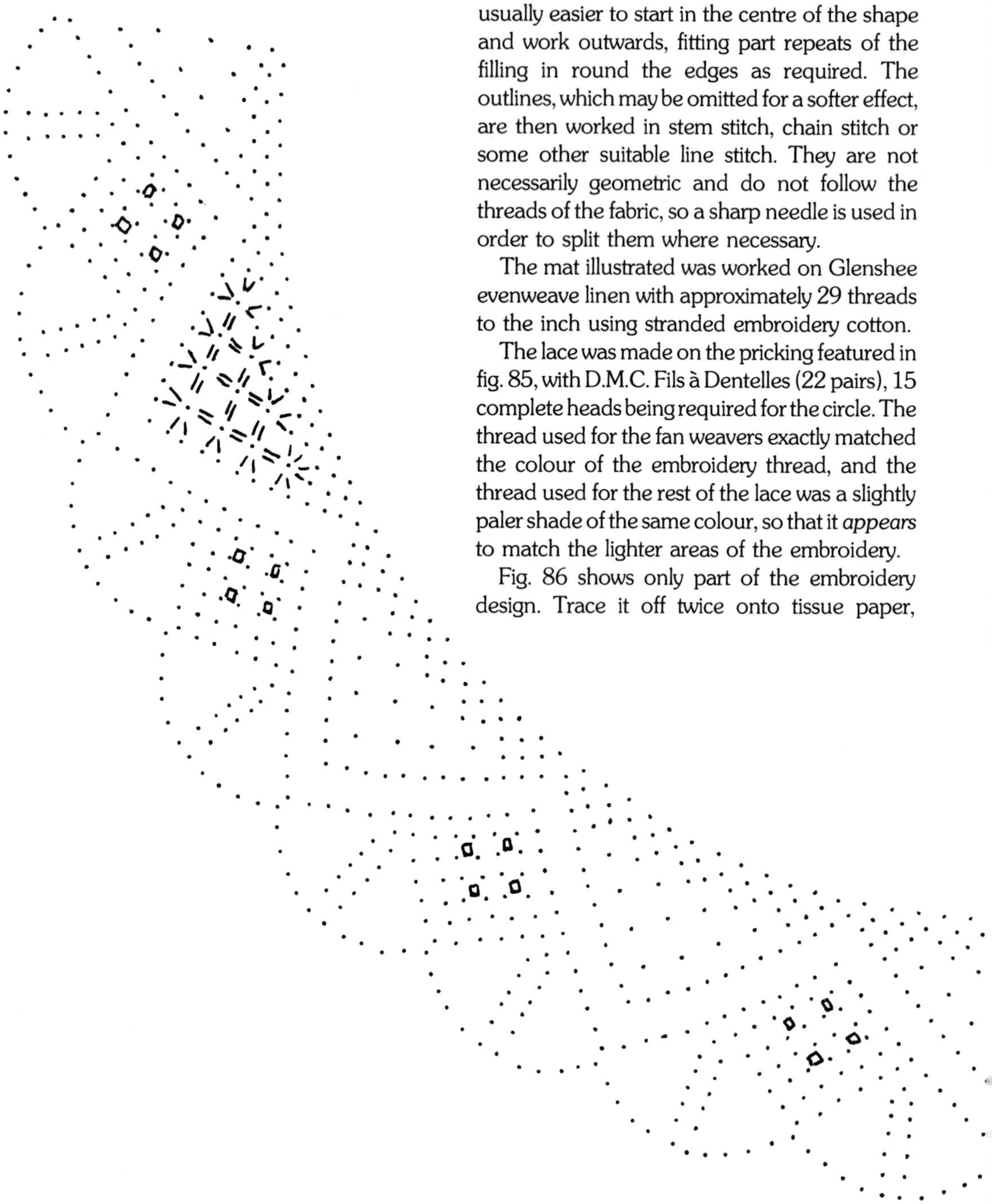

because they will tend to pull holes in the fabric and dark bits of fluff from the sewing thread may be left behind.

When working the fillings into a space it is usually easier to start in the centre of the shape and work outwards, fitting part repeats of the filling in round the edges as required. The outlines, which may be omitted for a softer effect, are then worked in stem stitch, chain stitch or some other suitable line stitch. They are not necessarily geometric and do not follow the threads of the fabric, so a sharp needle is used in order to split them where necessary.

The mat illustrated was worked on Glenshee evenweave linen with approximately 29 threads to the inch using stranded embroidery cotton.

The lace was made on the pricking featured in fig. 85, with D.M.C. Fils à Dentelles (22 pairs), 15 complete heads being required for the circle. The thread used for the fan weavers exactly matched the colour of the embroidery thread, and the thread used for the rest of the lace was a slightly paler shade of the same colour, so that it *appears* to match the lighter areas of the embroidery.

Fig. 86 shows only part of the embroidery design. Trace it off twice onto tissue paper, joining the two halves along the line A–B. Transfer the design to the fabric (see page 52) and then work the fillings. Those used for the mat are shown in fig. 87. Fillings (a), (b) and (c) were each worked with two strands of cotton, the shading being achieved by gradually omitting elements of the design as shown; (d), (e) and (f) were each worked with one, two and three strands of thread to achieve a gradual shading. The centre filling (g) was worked in two strands and it was outlined with stem stitch, again using two strands. The straight lines of the outline were also worked with two strands and the outer curved outline was worked with a single strand, stem stitch being used throughout.

The fabric was finished with a single bias strip cut from a fine matching linen (see page 34) and was hemmed invisibly into place. Be particularly careful to check that the embroidery is centrally placed.

Bands or motifs in blackwork, combined with lace would be ideal for table linen, whilst a skirt decorated with blackwork motifs and edged with lace would be very effective. Blackwork could also be worked down a sleeve, the cuff of which is trimmed with lace.

SHADOW WORK

A sheer fabric (e.g. organdie) is used for shadow work which results in a delicate appearance; it is therefore best combined with a fine lace. For the collar in fig. 88 a fine torchon lace was used, but many Bucks point type edgings would be ideal.

The embroidery is worked in double back stitch (see figs. 89 and 90) so that from the right side the design appears as two lines of back stitch with the thread which crosses between them on the wrong side, showing as a shadow between them. The designs are composed of pairs of lines or fairly narrow spaces which can be filled without leaving very long stitches on the reverse. Single lines, to link areas of the design, may be worked in back stitch.

The thread used should be fine to give a delicate result and may be white (on a white fabric) or coloured. Traditionally the fabric was white but it may be worthwhile to experiment

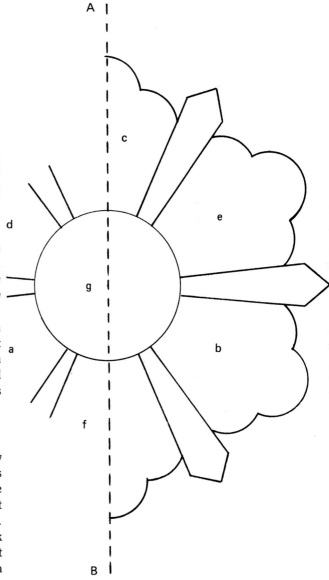

fig. 86 *Pattern for blackwork embroidery illustrated in fig. 84.*

69

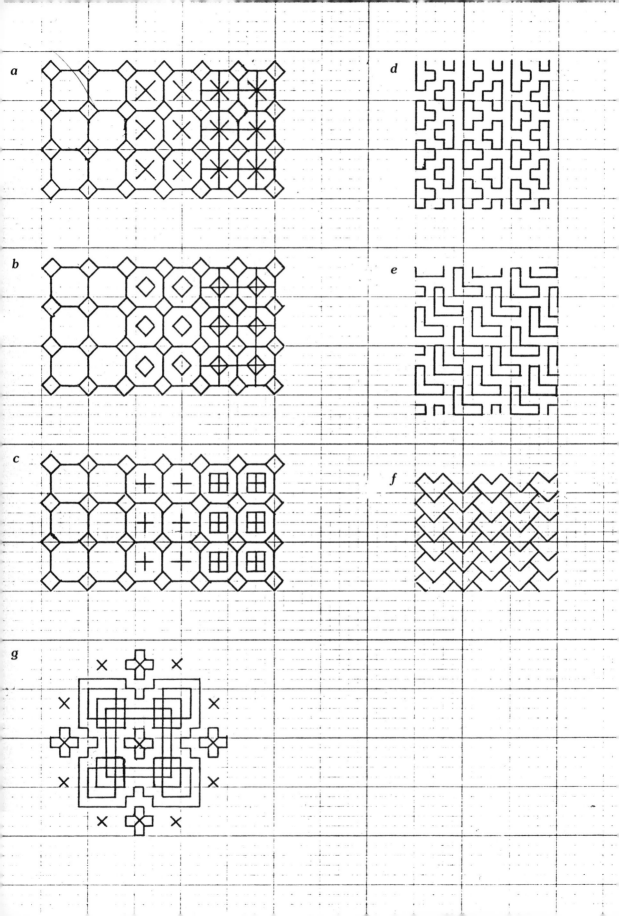

a

b

c

d

e

f

g

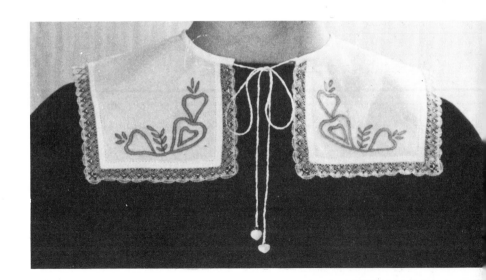

fig. 87 *Fillings for blackwork embroidery illustrated in fig. 84. Each square represents two threads of the fabric.*

fig. 88 *Collar combining shadow work and lace.*

fig. 89 *Detail of fig. 88 showing the embroidery and pin stitch through both layers of fabric.*

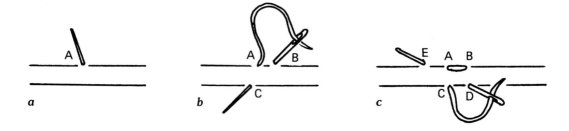

fig. 90 *Double back stitch:* **a** *Come up at A.* **b** *Go in at B and out at C.* **c** *Go in at D and out at E ready to start next stitch.*

with other colours. If a coloured thread is used the outline appears as a firm line, the shape appearing to be filled with a much paler tint of that colour.

When working, take great care not to carry the thread across the back of the work from one section to another because it will show. This makes it necessary to start and fasten off for each shape. To start the embroidery, leave an end of thread which can later be threaded into a needle and darned in to the back of the stitches where it should not show from the front. Finish off in the same way.

The embroidery on the collar illustrated was worked in a single strand of stranded embroidery cotton in a mid blue, and the white lace was made with Copley Marshall cotton No. 80/2 (13 pairs). To emphasize the half stitch hearts I used a single pair of gimp threads (D.M.C. Coton à broder No. 16) in a pale blue to echo the pale 'shadow' in the embroidery.

Before starting work on the collar, check the pattern size and adjust the neckline if necessary. The actual finished size of collar is shown in fig. 91. Trace off both sections and join them along the line A–B. Choose a pricking for a narrow lace (or see fig. 92) so that it may be eased round the slight curve on the side edge (this edge must be curved so that, when worn, the collar will appear square). Take rubbings of your chosen pricking and lay them in position round the edge of your collar pattern to check the number of repeats needed. It may be necessary to slightly alter your pattern to accommodate the lace.

fig. 91 *Pattern for collar illustrated in fig. 88. Trace off both sections and join A–B (no seams allowed).*

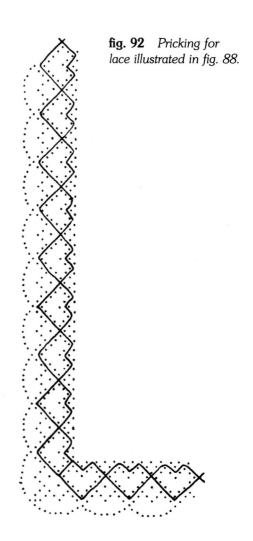

fig. 92 *Pricking for lace illustrated in fig. 88.*

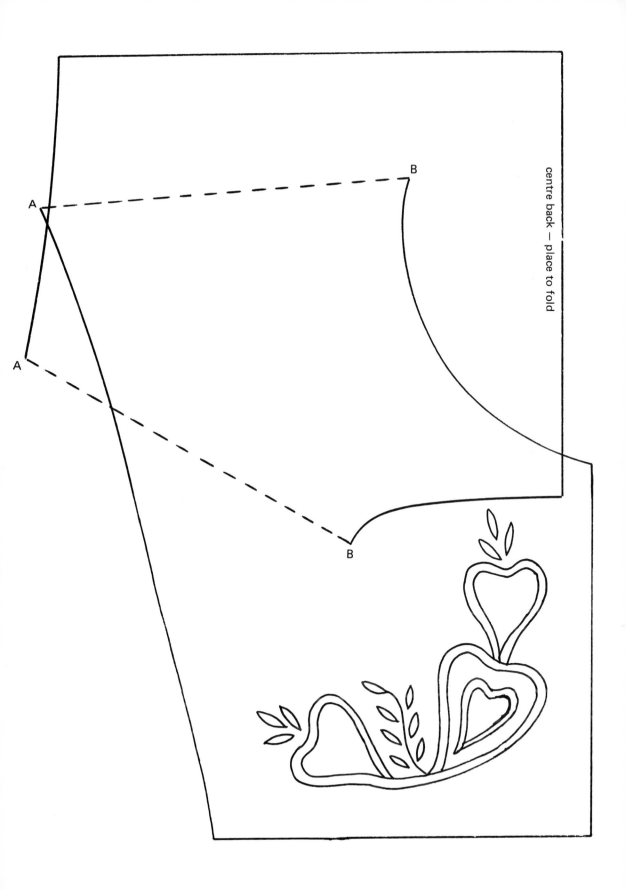

centre back — place to fold

Make the lace and then transfer the collar outline and embroidery design to the fabric (see page 52), checking that the lace will fit and that the embroidery is correctly positioned.

When the embroidery is complete, make up the collar as follows. Place the embroidered and backing fabrics together, right sides facing each other, and stitch them together on the seam line, leaving the neck edge open (a white cotton fabric was chosen for the backing in order to emphasize the shadow work). Trim the seams 5mm ($\frac{3}{16}$in.) from the stitching (leaving the neck edge at the moment), layer them and clip the corners (see figs. 43 and 45) and then turn the collar through to the right side, taking particular care with the corners. Press carefully before working a line of pin stitch to hold the two layers together round all the stitched edges. This pin stitching should be 5mm ($\frac{3}{16}$in.) in from the edges in order to disguise the turning which will show through to the right side (see fig. 89).

Tack the neck edges together and then oversew the lace into place. Now finish the neck edge with a strip of bias binding (about 39mm ($1\frac{1}{2}$in.) wide) cut from the backing fabric. Stitch the binding to the right side of the collar along the seam line, including the ends of the lace as shown in fig. 93a. Trim the seam to 5mm ($\frac{3}{16}$in.), layer it and then fold the binding over the seam as shown in fig. 93b, tucking in the raw edges and just covering the previous line of stitches. The finished binding should be about 7mm ($\frac{1}{4}$in.)

deep. Tuck in the raw edges at each end, level with the edge of the lace and stitch the binding neatly in place.

The finished collar may be stitched loosely into the neckline of the garment or be worn separately. In this case it could be fastened with a hook and bar or with ties. The neckline binding could be extended to form ties or they may be made from plaited threads. Those on the collar illustrated were made as follows: cut two 102cm (40in.) lengths of D.M.C. Perle No. 8, thread them through a bead as shown in fig. 94 with the bead at the centre and then use these four strands to make a half stitch plait of the required length. The four ends are all then knotted together and concealed in the neck binding.

CATHEDRAL WINDOW PATCHWORK

This type of patchwork is built up from a number of folded squares so that when completed there are no raw edges and the work does not need lining. Traditionally a variety of printed fabrics were used for the 'windows' but small lace motifs mounted on plain fabric can look very impressive.

The fabric is easier to handle if it will take a crease well, and, because of the amount of folding required, should not be too heavy. A dress-weight cotton is ideal, especially for a first attempt. Fabrics which will not crease readily may be used by tacking close to every fold as it is

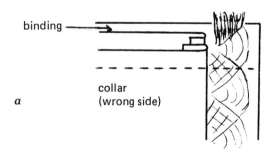
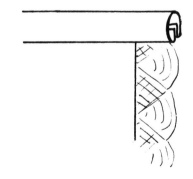

fig. 93 *a Stitch binding to right side of collar and across end of lace.* *b Fold binding over stitched line and end of lace.*

made; this will hold them accurately in place until the patchwork is finished, but involves a lot more work! Because of the folding which is involved, these squares use a surprisingly large amount of fabric.

The 'windows', which require only a small amount of material, should be cut from a fabric which will not fray easily, to avoid any danger of their pulling away. A fabric which does tend to fray should have its edges zig-zagged on the machine or overcast by hand after the windows have been cut.

The size of the windows is dependent on the size of the starting square for the blocks; for example a 179mm (7in.) square of fabric will make a block approximately 83mm (3¼in.) square and needs a window 54mm (2⅛in.) square, but a 215mm (8½in.) square of fabric forms a block 102mm (4in.) square and needs a window 68mm (2⅝in.) square.

If you need a specific size of window for your lace, experiment by folding paper to find the correct size (and remember to add 7mm (¼in.) extra all round before cutting the fabric). When planning, remember too that the lace will look its best if it has room to breathe and is not crammed close to the edges of the window.

To achieve good results, accurate cutting and folding is essential. Cut a square of the required size, allowing 7mm (¼in.) extra on each side for turnings. Press the turnings to the wrong side and then fold the square in half diagonally, pressing the fold to mark it. Open out the fabric and re-fold along the other diagonal, again pressing the fold. Open out the fabric with the wrong side facing you (see fig. 95a).

Now fold each corner in to the centre so that they meet there with the folded edges of the first square lying flat beside each other (see fig. 95b). Pin into place and then flat overcast the adjacent edges together so that all the raw edges have been enclosed. Take care when stitching not to catch in the lower layer of fabric and to make sure that the corners of the new, smaller, square are flat and true.

Keeping the square stitched side up, again fold in the corners to meet at the centre. Make

fig. 94 *Thread bead onto centre of two lengths of thread.*

two cross stitches, one on top of the other, right through all the layers of fabric to hold these corners in place (see fig. 95c). Use a fine, strong, matching thread and keep these stitches as small and neat as possible; they will be on the right side of the finished work and should be inconspicuous. This completes one block; the flat surface will be on the wrong side and the diagonal folds will be on the right side.

Complete the number of blocks required and then place two together, right sides facing. Overcast them together along one side, picking up only a couple of threads from each fold. Join on more blocks in the same way to make a strip of the required length. The remaining blocks are joined into similar strips which may then be joined to each other. At this stage the patchwork will look very uninspiring; it is at the next stage, the insertion of the windows, that it will suddenly appear almost finished.

The windows are placed in the diamond shapes which are formed between adjacent blocks by the folded diagonals (see shaded areas in fig. 95d). The fabric for the window, to which the lace is applied invisibly (see page 50), should be cut 4mm (⅛in.) smaller than this diamond.

Place the window into position, pin it in the four corners as shown in fig. 95e and then bring the diagonal folds forward to cover the edges of the window. The folds should lie next to each other in the corners for about 7mm (¼in.) and be arranged in an attractive curve (see fig. 95f).

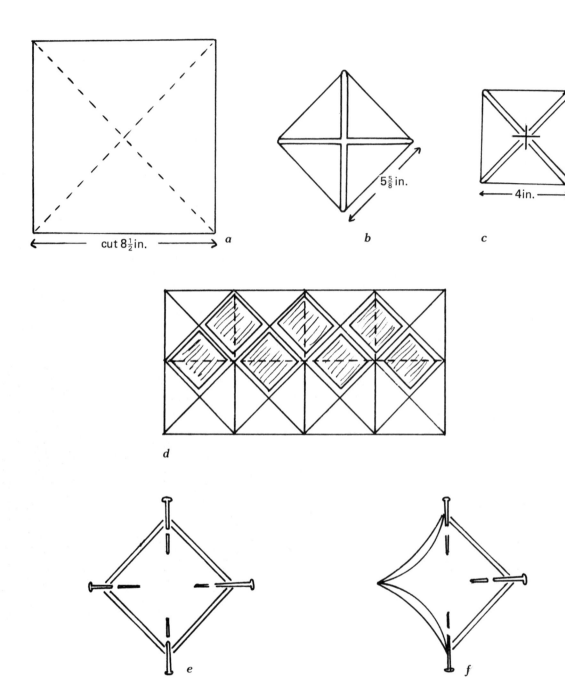

fig. 95 *a Cut 217mm (8½in.) square fabric. Press under 7mm (¼in.) all round to make 204mm (8in.) square. Crease to mark diagonals. b Fold each corner in to centre and flat overcast adjacent edges. c Fold each corner in to centre and hold with two cross stitches through all layers. d Eight blocks (two rows of four) joined. Shaded areas indicate position of two rows of windows. e Pin windows into position. f Fold edges over window and stitch.*

fig. 96 *Cushion in cathedral window patchwork with Honiton lace motifs. Actual size approximately 408mm (16in.) square.*

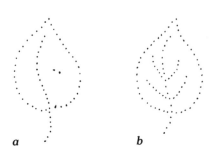

a   *b*

fig. 97 *Prickings for lace on cushion illustrated in figs. 96 and 98.* **a** *Worked as a divided leaf.* **b** *Worked with raised ribs and vein.*

fig. 98 *Detail of fig. 96. Note the folds of fabric meeting in the corner of the windows.*

fig. 99 *Pricking for lace on cushion illustrated in figs. 96 and 101.*

fig. 100 *Pricking for lace on cushion illustrated in figs. 96 and 101.*

fig. 101 *Detail of fig. 96.*

These folds are then slip-stitched invisibly together at the corners and to the fabric of the window along the sides, taking care that the stitching does not go through the other layers of fabric (see fig. 98).

To insert part windows at the edges (these are best left without any lace) treat them exactly as above, pinning the two folded edges into place. The third edge of the window may now be cut about 7mm ($\frac{1}{4}$in.) outside the finished edge of the block, the raw edge being tucked under, level with the edge of the block and enclosed between it and the window, which is stitched invisibly into place.

The cushion illustrated in fig. 96 was made from 16 blocks, starting with 215mm (8$\frac{1}{2}$in.) squares of fabric. The prickings for the lace, which were worked in George Wigley's No. 180 cotton, are given in figs. 97, 99 and 100 and are illustrated in figs 98 and 101. Needle-made lace motifs would also be ideal. The reverse of this cushion was quilted (see fig. 102).

To make up the cushion prepare a piping cord and stitch it to the quilted reverse as described on page 91. Because the patchwork has no raw edges or seam allowances, the method of making the cushion is different to that described on page 91. Trim the wadding from the seam allowance to reduce bulk and then turn the seam allowance to the back of the quilting so that the piping sits round the edge.

The cushion front is then placed in position over the quilting, wrong sides together, and stitched into place on the piping from the outside. Work in an invisible slip stitch round three sides, insert the cushion pad and then continue along the fourth side. This is fairly time-consuming but gives a very accurate finish. A zip could be included in one seam to allow for easy removal for laundering but would spoil the line of the cushion however neatly it was inserted.

QUILTING

Quilting is a monochrome technique, which relies for its effect on the shadows it casts. It is useful for making frames, being particularly good for Honiton-type motifs.

English (wadded) quilting is made up of three layers of fabric which are held together by the stitching that also forms the pattern. The backing fabric should be lightweight, muslin being a good choice. The middle layer is a wadding, Terylene (Dacron) being an ideal fabric because it is washable. Various thicknesses are available, but for use with lace it is usually better to make the quilting fairly thin. The top fabric should be smooth and soft; satin is a popular choice but

fig. 102 *Detail of quilted reverse of cushion shown in fig. 96.*

polyester/cotton mixtures work well and were used for both the frame and cushion illustrated in figs. 3 and 102.

The thread used should match the fabric exactly or be very slightly darker, an ordinary sewing thread being suitable.

The design may be transferred to the top fabric by either of the methods described on page 52, or the quilting may be worked directly through tissue paper. When planning quilting, remember that it does tend to 'shrink' the fabric, and this must be allowed for. If an accurate size is important, work samples, using the chosen materials and measuring them before and after working the quilting (the 'shrinkage' will to some extent depend on the thickness of wadding).

To prepare the fabrics for quilting, transfer the design to the top fabric (if required) and place it on top of the wadding and backing fabric as shown in fig. 103, making sure they all lie flat. If the design is to be worked directly through the tissue, put that in place on top of the uppermost fabric. Tack through all layers to prevent them from slipping, working from the centre, in the directions and order shown in fig. 104, making the lines about 51mm (2in.) to 78mm (3in.)

apart. If you are working in a frame then the backing fabric is framed (see page 53) before placing and tacking the other layers.

The quilting may then be worked in running stitch (for a soft line), back stitch (for a crisp line) or chain stitch (for a heavy line), always starting from the centre of the design. The quilting illustrated was worked in back stitch, with the filled areas in lines of running stitch.

The design for the cushion back was based on the cathedral window patchwork, and samples were worked to decide on the exact size. I found it necessary to add about 7mm ($\frac{1}{4}$in.) to the quilting fabric for each block of the cushion, but you should check with your own materials. The lace prickings were used as the patterns for the motifs.

It would be possible to apply motifs (see page 49) of fairly bold lace to the top fabric and then work quilting round them for an unusual jacket or waistcoat. Italian quilting would be ideal for use in this way; this is worked in a similar manner but omitting the layer of wadding. The designs are made up of parallel lines which form a channel into which thick wool is threaded from the back in order to pad them.

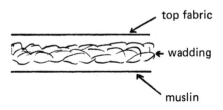

fig. 103 *Place the layers of fabric as shown.*

fig. 104 *Tack the layers together in the order and directions shown.*

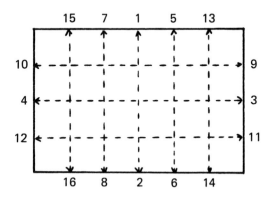

CHAPTER SEVEN

Ideas for Using Lace

Lace has always been used extensively in dress; edgings, frills and deep flounces have enjoyed repeated popularity. The comparatively simple fashions of today, and the need for easy laundering in a busy world, frequently demand something much simpler, although the lavish use of lace still has its place for special occasions. Beware though of too lavish a use of handmade lace, it is amazing how many people think that because there are yards of it, it cannot be handmade, and therefore overlook it! If the lace is being used in a traditional way, chapters 3 and 4 should provide the information you require.

Your lace may be used as an accessory or as part of a garment. If the lace forms part of the garment, choose a fairly classic simple style, which will show off the lace to advantage and remain fashionable for a reasonable length of time; after all, you will spend a great deal of time making it! Accessories may be added to both classic and high fashion garments as appropriate, and may also be used on different garments thus extending the useful life of the lace. They may also be added to ready-made garments, so it is not necessary to be a proficient dressmaker in order to wear lace.

When lace is used as part of a garment, remember that it will be easier to launder if it is applied and therefore fully supported. Effective use can be made of small amounts of lace but they must appear as an integral part of the garment, which should look incomplete without them.

BUTTONS

One method of gaining the maximum effect with the minimum of lace is to make lace-covered buttons. The lace may be of any suitable colour and in a scale to suit both the size of the button and the fabric of the garment. Two of these buttons could be joined back-to-back to form an attractive cufflink. Button moulds are available from haberdashers in a variety of sizes and full instructions for covering them are included in the pack. The main point to remember when using lace in this way is that it should be sewn onto a suitable fabric and the two layers then treated as one. This backing fabric may match the garment and the lace be a contrast, or vice versa. When choosing the fabric, do not overlook the fact that lace over a matching fabric can be extremely effective.

These buttons could be the only lace on the garment and may be used to replace those on a ready-made garment. Alternatively, they could be used as the final touch on a lace-trimmed garment. If this is the case, try to include some element of the lace design used for the trimming in that for the button (see fig. 105). A single spider, a 'flower' of leaves or a group of honeycomb buds, each surrounded by areas of ground, could all be possibilities. A piece worked in one stitch would be another idea, rose ground being one suitable choice (see fig. 106).

When making the lace it may be started and finished with knotted threads which will be hidden in the back of the mould. For the same reason the edges will not need careful attention. Do make sure that you make the piece large

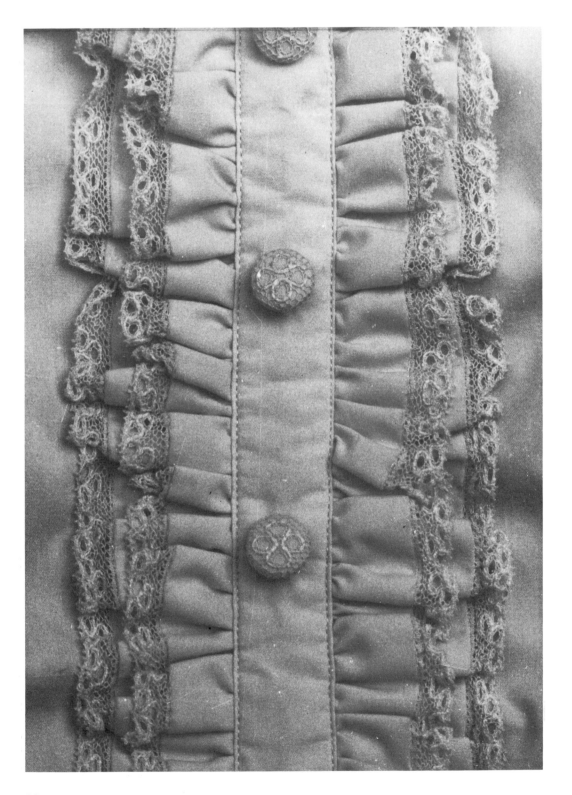

fig. 105 *Detail of blouse shown in fig. 110.
Note that the lace on the buttons (over a
matching fabric) echoes that on the frills.*

fig. 106 *Group of six buttons. Diameters
range from 17mm ($\frac{5}{8}$in.) to 28mm (1$\frac{1}{8}$in.).*

fig. 107 *Collar with Honiton lace edging (details in figs. 12 and 23).*

fig. 108 *Collar shown in fig. 107 worn the opposite way round.*

enough to secure the ends firmly in the mould; its size may be adjusted by the addition of more ground. When mounting the lace take particular care that it is correctly positioned on the mould. In order to position small lace motifs accurately, first cover the button mould with fabric and then stitch the lace into place.

COLLARS

Detachable collars are extremely useful, and whilst they may be composed entirely of lace they will be more serviceable if made of fabric and trimmed with lace. They may either be tacked loosely onto the garment or worn separately, fastened by ties or with a hook and bar (see page 74). They can be of a wide variety of shapes, and may be broad or narrow with either a simple lace edging, which may be flat or gathered, or with

very ornate lace (figs. 88, 107 and 108). On larger collars motifs could be applied or inserted. A collar made from a tiny print fabric could be effective with a lace edging made of a colour to pick out one of those in the print.

Collars which form part of the garment may also be trimmed with edgings or appliqués; a small motif applied in each corner of a mandarin collar could be extremely effective. These motifs could be continued all round the collar. Although these collars appear to be straight they are often curved, so that strips of lace applied to them would need to be shaped or eased gently into place. Garments with a tie collar could have the ends of the tie trimmed with an applied or inserted motif, or the ends may be finished with a lace edging.

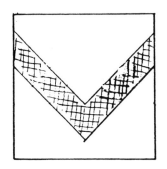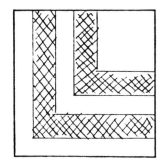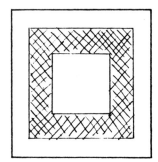

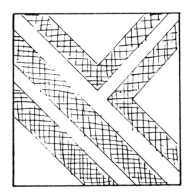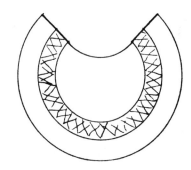

fig. 109 *Suggestions for patch pockets using applied or inserted lace.*

POCKETS

Pockets are another area in which lace can be effectively used. Patch pockets, in a variety of shapes, may have motifs applied or inserted (in this case they could be interlined with a contrasting fabric) or be edged with lace. Figs. 109 and 110 show a few ideas for using edgings or insertions on patch pockets.

Detachable pocket flaps are also very practical, being tacked into place inside the pocket. They can be a variety of shapes and may be

fig. 110 *Skirt with patch pockets trimmed with lace (see fig. 9). All frills on the blouse are edged with lace (see fig. 105).*

trimmed with edgings or insertions; semicircles, rectangles and triangles are all useful shapes (see fig. 111). The angles of triangles may be adjusted to suit the lace prickings, making for some easy Bucks point type corners.

SLEEVES AND CUFFS

A long sleeve may have a strip of lace inserted or applied down its length. Place the centre (widthways) of the lace at the shoulder seam and make sure the lace follows the straight grain of the fabric. This sleeve could be finished with a cuff to which lace may also be applied. The lace on the cuff can be the only lace on the garment and is particularly effective if the cuff is finished with a fabric frill. A more ornate cuff may be made in the same way by edging the frill with lace (see fig. 112).

YOKES AND SKIRTS

The yokes of garments can be emphasized and trimmed with either inserted or applied lace in a variety of ways; a few ideas are shown in fig. 113.

Skirts of garments are another possibility for carrying lace decoration. A band or bands of insertion can be applied round the hem, choosing a style of garment suitable for a border pattern. It is better not to use inserted lace in this situation because the weight of the hem could pull the lace out of shape (this idea could also be used on the hem of a curtain).

Strips of lace may be inserted or applied to run down a skirt. The centre of each gore of a six or eight gore skirt (along the straight grain of the fabric) would be a suitable place for the lace. If it is

fig. 111 *Pocket flap (wrong side shown in fig. 41).*

fig. 112 *Sleeve with cuff. Detail of frill shown in fig. 31. White lace edging with a golden yellow gimp. Applied lace is the same golden yellow.*

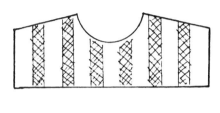

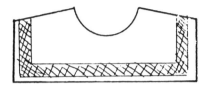

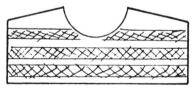

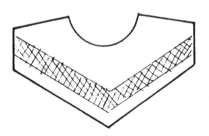

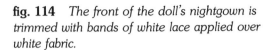

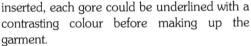

fig. 113 *Suggestions for trimming garment yokes with applied or inserted lace.*

fig. 114 *The front of the doll's nightgown is trimmed with bands of white lace applied over white fabric.*

inserted, each gore could be underlined with a contrasting colour before making up the garment.

The doll's nightgown in fig. 114 illustrates the use of short strips of applied lace (using very simple braids) to give a very rich effect and is relatively easy in construction because all the ends of the lace may be concealed in the seams. The same idea could be used on a child's christening gown or for a dress (especially for a bridesmaid) using wider laces. Corners of lace, arranged diagonally, may be used in a similar way. On a suitably shaped garment it could be used for a bridal gown or for an evening dress, especially if metallic threads are incorporated.

Similar ideas can also be used for a nightdress or underskirt. Lingerie has always been popular for decorating with lace in a variety of ways, but it does seem a shame to hide hand-made lace from the world!

BELTS

A lace trimmed belt can be very effective on an otherwise plain garment, the lace being either motifs or a strip. If the belt is made from the same fabric as the garment the lace will have most impact. The fastening should be as unobtrusive as possible. One way of doing this would be to make eyelets at both ends (using either button-hole stitch or bought metal eyelets) and lacing the belt to fasten it, or the eyelets could be replaced by rouleau loops of fabric (see fig. 115). Alternatively use a buckle without a prong, stitching one end of the fabric into place. The other end is then threaded into the buckle and fastened at the back with velcro as shown in fig. 116.

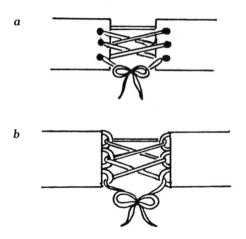

fig. 115 *Laced fastenings for belts.* *a Using metal or stitched eyelets.* *b Using rouleau loops.*

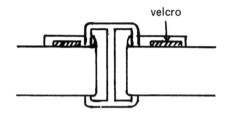

fig. 116 *Fastening a belt with a prongless buckle.*

HANDKERCHIEFS

Handkerchiefs have always been popular for trimming with lace, and whilst a deep edging of fine lace all round looks splendid, it represents a lot of work. For a more everyday handkerchief consider applying or inserting a lace motif near one corner (see pages 43 and 49); even the simplest laces can be very effective. They also make relatively easy (but impressive) gifts for non-lacemaking friends (see figs. 117 and 118).

There are a number of possibilities for finishing the outer hem of the fabric, but the method chosen should give a similar effect to that chosen for inserting the motif, in order to avoid a 'bitty' appearance. A single fold hem finished with two rows of four-sided stitch, a double fold hem pin-stitched into place or a neatly rolled hem (take care with the corners) are all possibilities. Another alternative would be to attach a very narrow lace braid all round, using one of the direct methods (see page 28). A motif could of course be applied to or inserted in a ready-made handkerchief to save time.

Roughly triangular pieces have always been popular on one corner of a handkerchief, and again there is more than one way of dealing with them. The fabric hem may be prepared all round, choosing the most suitable of the methods on pages 30 to 33, and the lace corner then oversewn into place. Alternatively the lace can be attached by one of the direct methods on pages 19 to 25, and the remaining hems then finished as before. Another idea would be to attach a very narrow lace braid all round by one of the direct methods, and then to attach the lace corner to this braid by flat overcasting.

TABLE LINEN

Lace may also be used for trimming household items, table linen being a popular choice. Table-cloths, traycloths and placemats can be extremely impressive but it is a long way round them when you come to make a complete lace edging, especially for a complete set of mats. They will also require very careful laundering. A more speedy, but still attractive, result will be obtained if the amount of lace can be reduced.

For the minimum effort, consider placing a motif in one corner (particularly for a placemat or traycloth). This motif can be applied or inserted (see pages 43 and 49) and if the fabric is finished with a simple drawn thread hem or a pin-stitched hem it can be most effective. Matching serviettes may be made by the same method. Strips of lace could be used in a similar way, many bookmark prickings being particularly suitable for adaption (see fig. 119).

A lace edging may be started and finished on a straight line if a suitable pricking is chosen. The lace can then be made to fit along the short sides of a mat or traycloth. The fabric would be best

fig. 117 *Three handkerchiefs. Details are shown in figs. 52, 57 and 61.*

finished with a drawn thread or pin-stitched hem and could be further decorated with drawn thread work or blackwork before overcasting the lace into place.

CUSHIONS

Cushion covers may be both attractive and practical if trimmed with lace. One idea would be to use cathedral window patchwork as shown in fig. 96, but other simpler ideas can be equally attractive. Straight strips of lace and drawn thread work may be combined and would be ideal for a first attempt at drawn thread work as there are no corners to cause problems. The ends of the lace do not need finishing, but can disappear into a seam.

Strips of lace and closed borders may be either inserted or applied in various arrangements. Fig. 120 illustrates one possibility and some of the suggestions for patch pockets in fig. 109 could be enlarged for cushion covers.

fig. 118 *Handkerchief with torchon lace edging. Actual size 306mm (12in.) square, including lace (detail in fig. 22).*

fig. 119 *Place mat with simple drawn thread hem and two strips of applied lace. Detail in fig. 60.*

fig. 120 *Cushion with inserted torchon lace. Details in figs. 55 and 59. Actual size 408mm (16in.) square.*

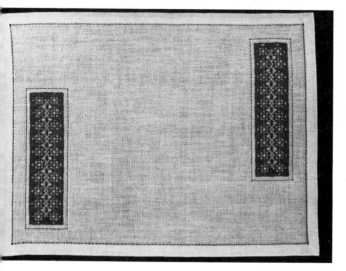

Make a cushion cover as follows, using a piping cord which must be washed before use to shrink it. Cut a bias strip of the fabric to the length required, joining it as shown in fig. 35. Its width should be the circumference of the cord plus 26mm (1in.) for seams. Enclose the cord as shown in fig. 121 and then, using the zipper foot on the machine, stitch as close to the cord as possible, stretching the fabric slightly as you stitch.

fig. 121 *Enclose the cord in bias strip and stitch.*

Cut out the cushion front allowing 13mm (½in.) seams all round and tack the piping cord into place, on the right side, as shown in fig. 122. Make sure all the raw edges are level and at the corners snip into the seam allowance on the binding covering the cord.

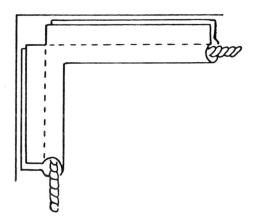

fig. 122 *Pin covered cord to cushion front, cutting fabric in corners as shown.*

To join the cord firstly undo a little of the stitching holding the binding in place. Make a seam in the binding, cutting away any excess and pressing the seam open. Now cut the cord so that the two ends butt up to each other, bind each end with thread to prevent unravelling and join by making stitches across the join as shown in fig. 123. The binding is then stitched back into place round the cord, tacked to the cushion front and machined into place all round the cushion, again using the zipper foot.

fig. 123 *Bind the cut ends of cord and stitch together as shown.*

To reduce bulk, avoid joining the cord and binding in exactly the same place.

The cushion front and back may now be joined, right sides together, around four corners and along three sides as shown in fig. 124. Use the zipper foot to stitch as close to the cord as possible. Turn the cushion to the right side, taking particular care with the corners, and insert the cushion pad. The opening may be closed by stitching neatly or by including a zip in this seam.

If the design of the cushion requires the ends

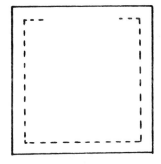

fig. 124 *Stitch front and back of cushion together where indicated by broken lines.*

of inserted lace to be enclosed in the seams then it must be interlined by tacking to a contrasting fabric *before* making up. If the design is similar to that of the cushion shown in fig. 120 then the pad may be covered with a coloured fabric.

LAMPSHADES

Lampshades can be trimmed with lace edgings and braids (including bobbin-made fringes) but there are further possibilities which may require less lace and be effective. Depending upon the lace and colours chosen the effect may be pretty or sophisticated. It is usually better to keep to the simpler styles of frame and choose a plain base.

Motifs or strips can be applied or inserted, although it is easier to handle applied pieces. Strips of lace combined with drawn thread work or pulled work can be effective on a drum shaped frame, with a contrasting coloured lining. Take particular care not to leave long stitches at the back of the work; they may not show through the lining but they almost certainly will when the lamp is on. Remember during planning that the effect when lit may be completely different. The lace will be thrown into silhouette so fairly bold shapes will be preferable. Beds/Maltese type laces would be particularly suitable and Honiton motifs could be effective. On a straight drum-shaped frame a border of Honiton flowers may be arranged to 'grow' up round the frame from the lower edge. For a child the same shape can be turned into a 'carousel' by 'suspending' suitably shaped animals by braid 'poles' from the top edge of the frame which is then finished with a suitable braid. This idea would lend itself to either Honiton or tape lace, or a combination of the techniques of each.

To make the shade, bind the frame with bias binding and then pin and stitch the top fabric into place. The lace may then be applied working in the same way as in an embroidery frame. The ends of the lace must *not* be darned to the back of the fabric; they would show when the frame is lit. The lining is then stitched into place and the upper and lower edges are finished with an appropriate braid.

Further Reading

A wide range of books on lacemaking and embroidery is available. The following are a few suggestions:

Ambuter, Carolyn. *The Open Canvas*, Penguin

Beaney, Jan. *Stitches – New Approaches*, Batsford

Butler, Anne. *Batsford Encyclopaedia of Embroidery Stitches*, Batsford

Cave, Oenone. *Linen Cut Work*, Vista, republished by Dover

Colby, Averil. *Quilting*, Batsford

Cox, Dorothy. *Making Lace with Little Grey Rabbit*, published by the author and available from her at 83 Padleys Lane, Burton Joyce, Nottingham NG14 5BW

Earnshaw, Pat. *Lace in Fashion*, Batsford

Fishburn, Angela. *Lampshades – Technique and Design*, Batsford

Fisher, Jennifer. *Braid Lace for Today*, Dryad Press

Fisher, Jennifer. *Torchon Lace for Today*, Dryad Press

Lorant, Tessa. *Hand and Machine Knitted Laces*, Batsford

Lovesey, Nenia. *Creative Design in Needlepoint Lace*, Batsford

Nottingham, Pamela. *The Technique of Bobbin Lace*, Batsford

Snook, Barbara. *Embroidery Stitches*, Dryad Press

Sorenson, Veronica. *Modern Lace Design*, Batsford

Mary Thomas' Dictionary of Embroidery Stitches, Hodder & Stoughton

Mary Thomas' Embroidery Book, Hodder & Stoughton

Anchor Manual of Needlework, Batsford

Suppliers

Mary Allen
Wirksworth
Derbyshire
DE4 4BN

*(Embroidery threads and
materials; some lace threads –
mail order service)*

Framecraft Miniatures Ltd
148/150 High Street
Aston
Birmingham

*(Range of gilt and silverware
suitable for mounting – mail
order service)*

Joan Kelly
39 Copeland Avenue
Tittensor
Stoke-on-Trent
Staffordshire
ST12 9JA

*(Wide range of lace threads
and general lace supplies –
mail order service)*

Mace and Nairn
89 Crane Street
Salisbury
Wilts

Seba Lace
76 Main Street
Addingham
Ilkley
West Yorks
LS29 0PL

(All lacemaking requisites)

A. Sells
49 Pedley Lane
Clifton
Shefford
Beds

*(All lacemaking requisites –
mail order service)*

C. & D. Springett
21 Hillmorton Road
Rugby
Warwicks

(Bobbin maker)

The Lace Guild
The Hollies
53 Audnam
Stourbridge
West Midlands
DY8 4AE

Frank Herring & Son
27 West High Street
Dorchester
DT1 1UP

(Pillows, bobbins, winders)

Stuart Johnson Lace Bobbins
The Stables
The Holloway
Market Place
Warwick

(Bobbins and pillows)

D. J. Hornsby
149 High Street
Burton Latimer
Kettering
Northants

*(All lacemaking requisites –
mail order service)*

Index